Early praise for *Node.js the Right Way*

Node.js the Right Way really is the right way to get a fast start with modern server-side JavaScript programming. It goes far beyond the basic mechanics of JavaScript and Node and shows you what really goes into making a quality server-side application.

➤ **Allen Wirfs-Brock**
   Project editor, ECMAScript Language Specification

If you're just getting started with Node, skip everything else—this is the only book you'll need.

➤ **Rick Waldron**
   Software engineer, Bocoup, LLC

Finally, a book that teaches that Node.js is much more than a bare-bones web-scale application server for hipsters.

➤ **Eric Redmond**
   Coauthor of *Seven Databases in Seven Weeks*

Node.js the Right Way is a great read that quickly demonstrates Node's flexibility and power. It's perfect for any JavaScript developer who's interested in exploring the world of server infrastructure.

➤ **Xavi Ramirez**
   Baydin, Inc.

Node.js the Right Way is the right book to read. Skipping "Hello World" in favor of applicable examples, Wilson delivers a comprehensive introduction that is detailed yet engaging.

➤ **Daniel Renfro**
  Lead software engineer at Vistaprint

This book is a fantastic way to explain Node. I even used some of Jim's example code in a personal project (especially Chapter 7).

➤ **Mitchell Foley**
  Software engineer at Google

Node.js the Right Way

Practical, Server-Side JavaScript That Scales

Jim R. Wilson

The Pragmatic Bookshelf

Dallas, Texas • Raleigh, North Carolina

Our Pragmatic courses, workshops, and other products can help you and your team create better software and have more fun. For more information, as well as the latest Pragmatic titles, please visit us at *http://pragprog.com*.

The team that produced this book includes:

Jacquelyn Carter (editor)
Candace Cunningham (copyeditor)
David J Kelly (typesetter)
Janet Furlow (producer)
Juliet Benda (rights)
Ellie Callahan (support)

Printed in the United States of America.
ISBN-13: 978-1-937785-73-4
Printed on acid-free paper.
Book version: P1.0—December 2013

Contents

Acknowledgments vii

Preface ix

1. **Getting Started** 1
   Node's Niche   2
   How Node Applications Work   3
   Aspects of Node.js Development   5
   Get Node.js   7

2. **Wrangling the File System** 9
   Programming for the Node.js Event Loop   10
   Spawning a Child Process   13
   Capturing Data from an EventEmitter   15
   Reading and Writing Files Asynchronously   17
   The Two Phases of a Node Program   20
   Wrapping Up   20

3. **Networking with Sockets** 23
   Listening for Socket Connections   24
   Implementing a Messaging Protocol   28
   Creating Socket Client Connections   31
   Testing Network Application Functionality   32
   Extending Core Classes in Custom Modules   35
   Wrapping Up   39

4. **Robust Messaging Services** 41
   Advantages of ØMQ   42
   Importing External Modules with npm   42
   Message-Publishing and -Subscribing   44
   Responding to Requests   48
   Routing and Dealing Messages   52

Clustering Node.js Processes   54
Pushing and Pulling Messages   59
Wrapping Up   62

5. **Accessing Databases** **65**
Advantages of CouchDB   66
Creating a Package   67
Making RESTful Requests   68
Importing Real Data   70
Unit Testing with Nodeunit   73
Throttling Node.js   75
Querying Data with Mapreduce Views   81
Wrapping Up   85

6. **Scalable Web Services** **87**
Advantages of Express   88
Serving APIs with Express   88
Writing Modular Express Services   91
RESTful APIs with Promises   94
Yielding Control with Generators   99
Using Generators with Promises   101
Wrapping Up   104

7. **Web Apps** **107**
Storing Express Sessions in Redis   108
Creating a Single-Page Web Application   110
Authenticating with Passport   113
Authorizing APIs with Custom Middleware   116
Creating Authenticated APIs   118
Client-Side MVC   120
Wrapping Up   125
Parting Thoughts   126

Acknowledgments

This was a surprisingly difficult book to write, and I couldn't have done it without a lot of help. I'm especially thankful for my editor, Jackie Carter—your thoughtful feedback made this book what it is today.

I'd also sincerely like to thank the whole team at The Pragmatic Bookshelf. Thanks for your kind patience while I figured out how to write this book. And thanks to the entire team, who worked so hard to polish this book and find all of my mistakes.

I'd like to thank all my reviewers. Your keen observations have helped make this book even more technically correct (the best kind of correct). In no particular order:

Daniel Rinehart	Gary Katsevman	Xavi Ramirez
Daniel Renfro	David LaPalomento	Mitch Foley
Jesse Streb	Jarrett Cruger	Trevor Burnham
	Eric Redmond	

And I want to thank my wonderful family, too. Ruthy, you are my inspiration; with your quiet perseverance, you can achieve anything. Emma and Jimmy, even though you're both growing up too fast, I can't wait to see all the great things you'll do.

For anyone I missed, I hope you'll accept my apologies. Any omissions were certainly not intentional.

Preface

Two big shifts are happening right now in the practice of writing software, and Node.js is at the forefront of both.

First, software is becoming increasingly asynchronous. Whether you're waiting for a Big Data job, interacting with end users, or simply responding to an API call, chances are you'll need asynchronous programming techniques.

Second, JavaScript has quietly become the world's standard virtual machine—in web browsers, modern NoSQL databases, and now on the server as well.

Node.js is right at the intersection of these trends, and it's ready to take off in a big way.

Why Node.js the Right Way

In March of 2010, I gave a lightning talk titled "Full-Stack JavaScript" at the NoSQL Boston conference. Back then, and even more so now, I knew that using JavaScript for every layer of the application stack was not only possible, but a great way to reduce software complexity.

The *Right Way* in this book's title refers to both the process of learning Node and the practice of writing Node.

Learning Node.js

As for any growing technology, there are lots of resources available for learning Node.js. Many are intently focused on serving up web resources. The web is great, but it's not enough, and it's not the whole story of Node.

Ruby is more than Rails, and Python is more than Django. Node.js is more than serving web content, and this book treats it that way.

Node.js the Right Way teaches you the core concepts you'll need to be an effective Node.js programmer, no matter what kinds of programs you need to write.

Writing Node.js

One thing I love about JavaScript is that there are seven ways to do anything. There's breathing room, where developers can explore and experiment and find better approaches to everything.

The community of Node developers, conventions in Node.js development, and even the semantics of the JavaScript language itself are all rapidly evolving. With eyes to the near future, the code examples and recommendations in this book reflect current best practices and standards.

What's in This Book

This book is for developers who want to learn how to write asynchronous JavaScript for the server using Node.js. Some prior JavaScript experience will help, but you don't have to be an expert.

Chapter 1, *Getting Started*, on page 1, introduces the Node.js event loop, explaining how it empowers Node to be highly parallel and single-threaded at the same time. This chapter also outlines the five aspects of Node.js development that frame each subsequent chapter and has some brief instructions on getting Node installed on your machine.

The remaining chapters each deal with a specific practical programming area.

Wrangling the File System

In Chapter 2, *Wrangling the File System*, on page 9, we'll get our first look at writing Node.js programs. If you've done any server-side programming in the past, chances are you've had to access a file system along the way. We'll start in this familiar domain, using Node's file-system tools to create asynchronous, nonblocking file utilities. You'll use Node's ubiquitous EventEmitter and Stream classes to pipe data, and you'll spawn and interact with child processes.

Networking with Sockets

We'll expand on those concepts while exploring Node's network I/O capabilities in Chapter 3, *Networking with Sockets*, on page 23. We'll create TCP servers and client programs to access them. We'll also develop a simple JSON-based protocol and a custom module for working with these messages. This will offer insight into Node application design and provide experience creating testable and fault-tolerant systems.

Robust Message-Passing

Then, in Chapter 4, *Robust Messaging Services*, on page 41, we'll branch away from the Node core and into the realm of third-party libraries. You'll use npm to import and build ØMQ (pronounced "Zero-M-Q")—a high-efficiency, low-latency library for developing networked applications. With ØMQ, we'll develop programs that communicate using several important patterns, such as publish/subscribe and request/response. We'll create suites of programs that work together in concert, and you'll learn the clustering tools to manage them.

Accessing Databases

Chapter 5, *Accessing Databases*, on page 65, introduces databases and how to interact with them asynchronously in Node. In particular, we'll work with CouchDB—a RESTful, JSON document database. You'll learn how to parse XML documents, throttle Node using a worker queue, and develop and run unit tests. The database we create in this chapter is the foundation for RESTful APIs you'll develop in later chapters.

Scalable Web Services

Node has fantastic support for writing HTTP servers, and in Chapter 6, *Scalable Web Services*, on page 87, we'll do exactly that. You'll use Express, a popular Node.js web framework for routing requests. We'll dive deeper into REST semantics, and you'll use objects called promises for managing asynchronous code flows. You'll also learn about a bleeding-edge feature of ECMAScript called generator functions, and how they couple with promises in interesting ways.

Web Apps

Finally, in Chapter 7, *Web Apps*, on page 107, we'll build a front end for our web services. We'll use a Node module called Passport for implementing authenticated APIs that use Google account credentials. And we'll serialize our session data in Redis—a very fast key/value datastore. You'll learn the basics of writing a static single-page web application that uses RESTful APIs, including how to pull in dependencies using a front-end package manager called Bower.

What This Book Is Not

Before you commit to reading this book, you should know what it doesn't cover.

Everything About Everything

At the time of this writing, npm houses more than 43,000 modules, with an average growth rate of 100-plus new modules per day.[1] Since the ecosystem and community around Node.js is growing and changing so rapidly, this book does not attempt to cover everything. Instead, this short book teaches you the essentials you need to get out there and start coding.

The book also stays close to the topic of Node.js. You'll learn a lot about clustering Node processes and how to write scalable web services, but little about front-end concerns like HTML, CSS, and browser JavaScript.

JavaScript Beginner's Guide

The JavaScript language is one of the most misunderstood languages in wide use today. Although this book does discuss language syntax from time to time (especially where it's brand-new), this is not a beginner's guide to JavaScript.

A Note to Windows Users

The examples in this book assume you're using a Unix-like operating system. We'll make use of standard input and output streams, and pipe data between processes. The shell session examples have been tested with Bash, but other shells may work as well.

If you run Windows, I recommend setting up Cygwin.[2] This will give you the best shot at running the example code successfully, or you could run a Linux virtual machine.

Code Examples and Conventions

The code examples in this book contain JavaScript, shell sessions, and a few HTML/XML excerpts. For the most part, code listings are provided in full—ready to be run at your leisure.

Samples and snippets are syntax-highlighted according to the rules of the language. Shell commands are prefixed by $.

When you write Node.js code, you should always handle errors and exceptions, even if you just rethrow them. You'll learn how to do this throughout the book. However, some of the code examples lack error handling. This is to aid readability and save space only—you should always handle your errors.

---

1. http://www.modulecounts.com/
2. http://cygwin.com/

Online Resources

The Pragmatic Bookshelf's page for this book is a great resource.[3] You'll find downloads for all the source code presented in this book, and feedback tools, including a community forum and an errata-submission form.

Thanks for choosing this book to show you Node.js *the right way*.

Jim R. Wilson (jimbojw, hexlib)
November 2013

---

3.   http://pragprog.com/book/jwnode/node-js-the-right-way

CHAPTER 1

Getting Started

A lot of the buzz around Node.js is focused on the Web. In truth, Node serves a bigger purpose that people often miss. Let's see where Node fits in the broader scheme of things by making a map.

Imagine the universe of all possible programs as an immense sea. Programs that have similar purposes are near to each other, and programs that differ are further apart. With that picture in mind, take a look at the following figure. It shows a close-up of one particular outcrop in this sea, the Island of I/O-Bound Programs.

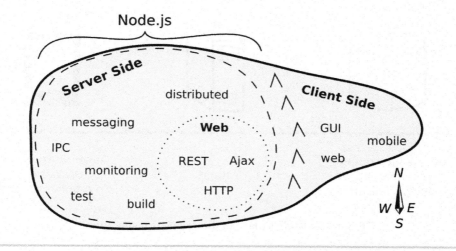

Figure 1—Map of the Island of I/O-Bound Programs

I/O-bound programs are constrained by data access. These are programs where adding more processing power or RAM often makes little difference.

East of the mountain range, we find the *client-side* programs. These include GUI tools of all stripes, consumer applications, mobile apps, and web apps. Client-side programs interact directly with human beings, often by waiting patiently for their input.

West of the mountains are the *server-side* programs. This vast expanse is Node.js territory.

Deep within the server-side region lies the Web—that old guard of HTTP, Ajax, REST, and JSON. The websites, apps, and APIs that consume so much of our collective mental energy live here.

Because we spend so much time thinking about the Web, we overemphasize Node's use in developing web applications. People ask, "How is Node better for making web apps?" or, "How can I make a REST service with Node?"

These are good questions, but they miss the point. Node is great for a wider range of things, and this book explores that larger world.

Node's Niche

Since JavaScript's first appearance in 1995, it has been solving problems all along the front-end/back-end spectrum. The following figure shows this spectrum and where Node.js fits within it.

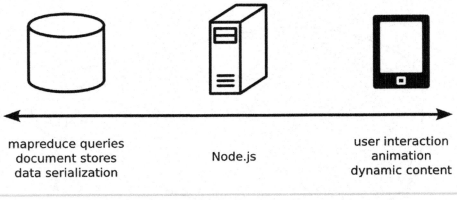

mapreduce queries		user interaction
document stores	Node.js	animation
data serialization		dynamic content

Figure 2—Node's place in the JavaScript spectrum

In the web browser on the right, much of the scripting involves waiting for user interaction. Click here, drag that, choose a file, etc. JavaScript has been extraordinarily successful in this space.

On the left, back-end databases are investing heavily in JavaScript. Document-oriented databases like MongoDB and CouchDB use JavaScript extensively —from modifying records to ad-hoc queries and mapreduce jobs. Other datastores, like Neo4j and Elasticsearch, present data in JavaScript Object Notation (JSON). These days, you can even write SQL functions for Postgres in JavaScript with the right plug-in.

Many middleware tasks are I/O-bound, just like client-side scripting and databases. These server-side programs often have to wait for things like a database result, feedback from a third-party web service, or incoming connection requests. Node.js is designed for exactly these kinds of applications.

How Node Applications Work

Node.js couples JavaScript with an *event loop* for quickly dispatching operations when events occur. Many JavaScript environments use an event loop, but it is a core feature of Node.js.

Node's philosophy is to give you low-level access to the event loop and to system resources. Or, in the words of core committer Felix Geisendörfer, in Node "everything runs in parallel except your code."[1]

If this seems a little backwards to you, don't worry. The following figure shows how the event loop works.

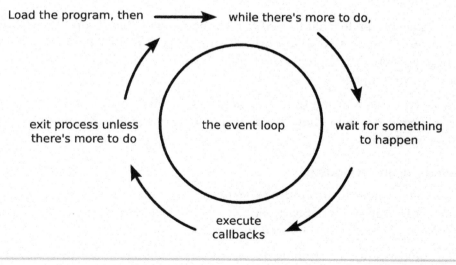

Figure 3—The Node.js event loop

---

1. http://www.debuggable.com/posts/understanding-node-js:4bd98440-45e4-4a9a-8ef7-0f7ecbdd56cb

As long as there's something left to do, Node's event loop will keep spinning. Whenever an *event* occurs, Node invokes any *callbacks* (event handlers) that are listening for that event.

As a Node developer, your job is to create the callback functions that get executed in response to events. Any number of callbacks can respond to any event, but only one callback function will ever be executing at any time.

Everything else your program might do—like waiting for data from a file or an incoming HTTP request—is handled by Node, in parallel, behind the scenes. Your application code will never be executed at the same time as anything else. It will always have the full attention of Node's JavaScript engine while it's running.

Single-Threaded and Highly Parallel

Other systems try to gain parallelism by running lots of code at the same time, typically by spawning many threads. But not Node.js. For JavaScript, Node is a single-threaded environment. At most, only one line of your code will ever be executing at any time.

Node gets away with this by doing most I/O tasks using *nonblocking* techniques. Rather than waiting line-by-line for an operation to finish, you create a callback function that will be invoked when the operation eventually succeeds or fails.

Your code should do what it needs to do, then quickly hand control back over to the event loop so Node can work on something else. We'll develop practical examples of this throughout the book, starting in Chapter 2, *Wrangling the File System*, on page 9.

If it seems strange to you that Node achieves parallelism by running only one piece of code at a time, that's because it is. It's an example of something I call a backwardism.

Backwardisms in Node.js

A *backwardism* is a concept that's so bizarre that at first it seems completely backwards. You've probably experienced many backwardisms while learning to program, whether you noticed them or not.

Take the concept of a *variable*. In algebra it's common to see equations like "$7x + 3 = 24$." Here, x is called a variable; it has exactly one value, and your job is to figure out what that value is.

Then when you start learning how to program, you quickly run into statements like "x = x + 7." Now x is still called a variable, but it can have any value that you assign to it. It can even have different values at different times.

From algebra's perspective, this is a backwardism. The equation "x = x + 7" makes no sense at all. The notion of a variable in programming is not just a little different—it's 100 percent backwards. But once you understand the concept of *assignment*, the programming variable makes perfect sense.

So it is with Node's single-threaded event loop. From a multithreaded perspective, running just one piece of code at a time seems silly. But once you understand event-driven programming—with nonblocking APIs—it becomes clear.

Programming is chock-full of backwardisms like these, and Node.js is no exception. Starting out, you'll frequently run into code that looks like it should work one way, but it actually does something quite different.

That's OK! With this book, you'll learn Node by making compact programs that interact in useful ways. As we run into more of Node's backwardisms, we'll dive in and explore them.

Aspects of Node.js Development

Node.js is a surprisingly big subject, so let's break it down into different *aspects*. There are many aspects of Node.js development we might talk about, ranging from basic JavaScript syntax to revision control. This book focuses on five in particular:

- Practical programming
- Architecture and core
- Patterns
- JavaScriptisms
- Supporting code

Let's explore each of these briefly.

Practical Programming

Practical programming is all about producing real code that does something useful. Interacting with a file system, establishing socket connections, or serving web applications are all examples of practical programming.

Each of the remaining chapters of this book focuses on one particular practical domain. Through code examples specific to each domain, you'll learn Node's architecture, patterns, JavaScriptisms, and supporting code.

Architecture and Core

Understanding Node's architecture will help you to harness its features while avoiding performance-crushing pitfalls. For example, Node uses an event loop written in C for scheduling work. But it executes application code in a JavaScript environment. How information is shuttled between these layers is the kind of impactful architectural detail you'll learn.

Patterns

Like any successful codebase with a healthy ecosystem, Node.js has a number of repeating patterns. Some of these patterns are baked into the core while others mostly appear in third-party libraries. Examples include the use of callbacks, error-handling techniques, and classes like EventEmitter and Stream, which are used liberally for event dispatching.

As we progress through different practical programming domains, we'll naturally encounter these and other patterns. When we do, you'll discover why they're useful and how to use them effectively.

JavaScriptisms

JavaScript is the language of Node programs, so you'll be seeing quite a lot of it. The code examples in this book make use of the latest available JavaScript features. Some of these features may be unfamiliar to you, even if you've done JavaScript development before.

JavaScriptisms discussed in this book include things like the nature of functions and object inheritance. ECMAScript Harmony—the code name for the next version of the JavaScript spec—packs some new features we'll use, too.

Supporting Code

Code does not live in isolation; it takes a village to support any individual program. Supporting code covers lots of things, from unit testing to performance benchmarks to deployment scripts. We'll use supporting code throughout the book to make our programs more robust, more scalable, and more manageable.

With these five aspects, you'll be able to develop applications that make the most use out of the platform while using idiomatic Node.js style. The example applications you'll develop in this book are functional and small, and aim to clearly demonstrate the five aspects. But to use them, you'll need to get Node.js installed first.

Get Node.js

To install Node.js, you have several choices based on your operating system and your comfort with building from source code.

This book assumes you're using the latest stable version of Node.js. If you install a different version—for example, by building from the latest source code—the code examples in this book may not work. From the command line you can run node --version to see what version you have installed if you're not sure.

```
$ node --version
v0.10.20
```

The easiest way to get Node is to download an installer from nodejs.org.[2]

Another popular option is Node Version Manager (nvm).[3] If you're using a Unix-like OS (like Mac OS X or Linux), you can install nvm like so:

```
$ curl https://raw.github.com/creationix/nvm/master/install.sh | sh
```

Then install a specific version:

```
$ nvm install v0.10.20
```

If you have trouble, you can get help on the Node mailing lists and IRC channel, both linked from the Node.js community page.[4]

We've got a lot of ground to cover, and we don't have many pages to do it. So if you're ready, let's begin in the oh-so-familiar domain of file-system access.

---

2. http://nodejs.org/download/
3. https://github.com/creationix/nvm
4. http://nodejs.org/community/

CHAPTER 2

Wrangling the File System

As a programmer, chances are you've had to access a file system at some point: reading files, writing files, renaming and deleting files. We'll start our Node.js journey in this familiar area, creating useful, asynchronous file utilities. Along the way we'll explore the following aspects of Node development.

Architecture and Core

On the architecture front, you'll see how the event loop shapes a program's flow. We'll use buffers for transporting data between Node's JavaScript engine and its native core, and we'll use Node's module system to bring in core libraries.

Patterns

Inside our programs, we'll use common Node patterns like callbacks for handling asynchronous events. We'll harness Node's EventEmitter and Stream classes to pipe data around.

JavaScriptisms

We'll take a look at some JavaScript features and best practices like "functions as first-class citizens" and block scoping.

Supporting Code

You'll learn how to spawn and interact with child processes, capture their output, and detect state changes.

We'll begin by creating a tool that watches a file for changes. This will give you a peek into how the event loop works while introducing Node's file-system APIs.

Programming for the Node.js Event Loop

Let's get started by developing a couple of simple programs that watch files for changes and read arguments from the command line. Even though they're short, these applications offer insights into Node's event-based architecture.

Watching a File for Changes

Watching files for changes is a convenient problem to start with because it demands asynchronous coding while demonstrating important Node concepts. Taking action whenever a file changes is just plain useful in a number of cases, ranging from automated deployments to running unit tests.

Open a terminal to begin. On the command line, navigate to an empty directory. You'll use this directory for all of the code examples in this chapter. Once there, use the touch command to create a file called target.txt.

```
$ touch target.txt
```

This file will be the target for our watcher program. Now open your favorite text editor and enter the following:

```
file-system/watcher.js
const fs = require('fs');
fs.watch('target.txt', function() {
  console.log("File 'target.txt' just changed!");
});
console.log("Now watching target.txt for changes...");
```

Save this file as watcher.js in the same directory as target.txt. Let's see how this program works.

First, notice the const keyword at the top. This JavaScriptism (part of ECMAScript Harmony) sets up a variable with a constant value. The require() function pulls in a Node *module* and returns it. In our case, we're calling require('fs') to incorporate Node's built-in file-system module.[1]

In Node.js, a module is a self-contained bit of JavaScript that provides functionality to be used elsewhere. The output of require() is usually a plain old JavaScript object. There's nothing particularly special about it, aside from the functionality provided by the module.

Node's module implementation is based on the CommonJS module specification.[2] Modules can depend on other modules, much like libraries in other

---

1. http://nodejs.org/api/fs.html
2. http://wiki.commonjs.org/wiki/Modules/1.1

programming environments, which import or #include other libraries. In Chapter 3, *Networking with Sockets*, on page 23, you'll learn how to create your own modules.

Next we call the fs module's watch() method, which polls the target file for changes and invokes the supplied callback function whenever it does.

In JavaScript, functions are first-class citizens. This means they can be assigned to variables and passed as parameters to other functions. Our callback function is an *anonymous* function; it doesn't have a name.

The callback function calls console.log() to echo a message to standard output whenever the file changes. Let's try it out.

Return to the command line and launch the watcher program using node, like so:

```
$ node --harmony watcher.js
Now watching target.txt for changes...
```

The --harmony parameter tells Node to use the latest ECMAScript Harmony features available. ECMAScript Harmony is the code name for the next version of ECMAScript, the standard behind the JavaScript language. Not all Harmony features are ready for prime time, but the ones we'll use in this book are OK (except where noted).

After the program starts, Node will patiently wait until the target file is changed. To trigger a change, open another terminal to the same directory and touch the file again:

```
$ touch target.txt
```

The terminal running watcher.js will output the string *File 'target.txt' just changed!*, and then the program will go back to waiting.

Visualizing the Event Loop

The program we wrote in the last section is a good example of the Node event loop at work. Recall the event-loop figure from *How Node Applications Work*, on page 3. Our simple file-watcher program causes Node to go through each of these steps, one by one.

To run the program, Node does the following.

1. It loads the script, running all the way through to the last line, which produces the *Now watching* message in the console.

2. It sees that there's more to do, because of the call to watch().

3. It waits for something to happen, namely for the fs module to observe a change to the file.

4. It executes our callback function when the change is detected.

5. It determines that the program still has not finished, and resumes waiting.

Node.js programs go through these steps, then the event loop spins until either there's nothing left to do or the program exits by some other means. For example, if an exception is thrown and not caught, the process will exit. We'll see how this works next.

Reading Command-Line Arguments

Now let's make our program more useful by taking in the file to watch as a command-line argument. This will introduce the process global object and how Node deals with exceptions.

Open your editor and enter this:

file-system/watcher-argv.js

```
const
  fs = require('fs'),
  filename = process.argv[2];
if (!filename) {
  throw Error("A file to watch must be specified!");
}
fs.watch(filename, function() {
  console.log("File " + filename + " just changed!");
});
console.log("Now watching " + filename + " for changes...");
```

Save the file as watcher-argv.js. You can run it like so (note the target.txt argument at the end):

```
$ node --harmony watcher-argv.js target.txt
Now watching target.txt for changes...
```

You should see the same output and behavior as the first watcher.js program. After outputting *Now watching target.txt for changes...* the script will diligently wait for changes to the target file.

This program uses process.argv to access the incoming command-line arguments. argv stands for *argument vector*; it's an array containing node and the full path to the watcher-argv.js as its first two elements. The third element (that is, at index 2) is target.txt, the name of our target file.

Notice that if a target file name is not provided the program will throw an exception. You can try that by simply omitting the target.txt parameter:

```
$ node --harmony watcher-argv.js
```

```
/full/path/to/script/watcher-argv.js:7
     throw Error("A file to watch must be specified!");
           ^
Error: A file to watch must be specified!
```

Any unhandled exception thrown in Node will halt the process. The exception output shows the offending file, and the line number and position of the exception.

Processes are important in Node. It's pretty common in Node development to spawn separate processes as a way of breaking up work, rather than putting everything into one big Node program. In the next section, you'll learn how to spawn a process in Node.

Spawning a Child Process

Let's enhance our file-watching example program even further by having it spawn a child process in response to a change. To do this, we'll bring in Node's child-process module and dive into some Node patterns and classes. You'll also learn how to use streams to pipe data around.

To keep things simple, we'll make our script invoke the ls command with the -lh options. This will give us some information about the target file whenever it changes. You can use the same technique to spawn other kinds of processes, as well.

Open your editor and enter this:

file-system/watcher-spawn.js

```
"use strict";
const
  fs = require('fs'),
  spawn = require('child_process').spawn,
  filename = process.argv[2];

if (!filename) {
  throw Error("A file to watch must be specified!");
}

fs.watch(filename, function() {
  let ls = spawn('ls', ['-lh', filename]);
  ls.stdout.pipe(process.stdout);
});
console.log("Now watching " + filename + " for changes...");
```

Save the file as watcher-spawn.js and run it with node as before:

```
$ node --harmony watcher-spawn.js target.txt
Now watching target.txt for changes...
```

If you go to a different console and touch the target file, your Node program will produce something like this:

```
-rw-r--r--  1 jimbo  staff      0B Dec 19 22:45 target.txt
```

The username, group, and other aspects of the file will be different from the preceding output, but the format should be the same.

The program we just made begins with the string "use strict" at the top. Strict mode was introduced in ECMAScript version 5—it disables certain problematic JavaScript language features and makes others throw exceptions. Generally speaking, it's a good idea to use strict mode.

Strict mode is also required to use certain ECMAScript Harmony features in Node, such as the let keyword. Like const, let declares a variable, but a variable declared with let can be assigned a value more than once.

Keep in mind that by using Harmony features (like let), your code will require the --harmony flag until these features become enabled by default. For example, const is already available without the --harmony flag, but not so for let.

Next, notice that we added a new require() at the beginning of the program. Calling require('child_process') returns the child process module. We're only interested in the spawn() method, so we save that to a constant with the same name and ignore the rest of the module.

```
spawn = require('child_process').spawn,
```

Remember, functions are first-class citizens in JavaScript, so we're free to assign them directly to variables like we did here.

Next, take a look at the callback function we passed to fs.watch().

```
function() {
  let ls = spawn('ls', ['-lh', filename]);
  ls.stdout.pipe(process.stdout);
}
```

The first parameter to spawn() is the name of the program we wish to execute; in our case it's ls. The second parameter is an array of command-line arguments. It contains the flags and the target file name.

The object returned by spawn() is a ChildProcess.[3] Its stdin, stdout, and stderr properties are Streams that can be used to read or write data. We want to send the

---

3.   http://nodejs.org/api/child_process.html

standard output from the child process directly to our own standard output stream. This is what the pipe() method does.

Sometimes you'll want to capture data from a stream, rather than just piping it forward. Let's see how to do that.

Capturing Data from an EventEmitter

EventEmitter is a very important class in Node.[4] It provides a channel for events to be dispatched and listeners notified. Many objects you'll encounter in Node inherit from EventEmitter, like the Streams we saw in the last section.

Now let's modify our previous program to capture the child process's output by listening for events on the stream. Open an editor to the watcher-spawn.js file from the previous section, then find the call to fs.watch(). Replace it with this:

file-system/watcher-spawn-parse.js
```
fs.watch(filename, function() {
  let
    ls = spawn('ls', ['-lh', filename]),
    output = '';
  ls.stdout.on('data', function(chunk){
    output += chunk.toString();
  });

  ls.on('close', function(){
    let parts = output.split(/\s+/);
    console.dir([parts[0], parts[4], parts[8]]);
  });
});
```

Save this updated file as watcher-spawn-parse.js. Run it as usual, then touch the target file in a separate terminal. You should see output something like this:

```
$ node --harmony watcher-spawn-parse.js target.txt
Now watching target.txt for changes...
[ '-rw-r--r--', '0B', 'target.txt' ]
```

The new callback starts out the same as before, creating a child process and assigning it to a variable called ls. It also creates an output variable, which will buffer the output coming from the child process.

Next we add *event listeners*. An event listener is a callback function that is invoked when an event of a specified type is dispatched. Since the Stream class inherits from EventEmitter, we can listen for events from the child process's standard output stream.

4.　http://nodejs.org/api/events.html

```
ls.stdout.on('data', function(chunk){
  output += chunk.toString();
});
```

The on() method adds a listener for the specified event type. We listen for data events because we're interested in data coming out of the stream.

Events can send along extra information, which arrives in the form of parameters to the callbacks. Data events in particular pass along a buffer object.[5] Each time we get a chunk of data, we append it to our output.

A *Buffer* is Node's way of representing binary data. It points to a blob of memory allocated by Node's native core, outside of the JavaScript engine. Buffers can't be resized and they require encoding and decoding to convert to and from JavaScript strings.

Calling toString() explicitly converts the buffer's contents to a JavaScript string using Node's default encoding (UTF-8). This means copying the content into Node's heap, which can be a slow operation, relatively speaking. If you can, it's better to work with buffers directly, but strings are more convenient.

Like Stream, the ChildProcess class extends EventEmitter, so we can add listeners to it, as well.

```
ls.on('close', function(){
  let parts = output.split(/\s+/);
  console.dir([parts[0], parts[4], parts[8]]);
});
```

After a child process has exited and all its streams have been flushed, it emits a close event. When the callback printed here is invoked, we parse the output data by splitting on sequences of one or more whitespace characters (using the regular expression /\s+/). Finally, we use console.dir() to report on the first, fifth, and ninth fields (indexes 0, 4, and 8), which correspond to the permissions, size, and file name, respectively.

We've seen a lot of Node's features in this small problem space of file-watching. You now know how to use key Node classes, including EventEmitter, Stream, ChildProcess, and Buffer. You also have firsthand experience writing asynchronous call-back functions and coding for the event loop.

Let's expand on these concepts in the next phase of our file-system journey: reading and writing files.

---

5.   http://nodejs.org/api/buffer.html

Reading and Writing Files Asynchronously

Earlier in this chapter, we wrote a series of Node programs that could watch files for changes. Now let's explore Node's methods for reading and writing files. Along the way we'll see two common error-handling patterns in Node: error events on EventEmitters and err callback arguments.

There are a few different approaches to reading and writing files in Node. The simplest way is to read in or write out the entire file at once. This technique works well for small files. Other approaches read and write by creating Streams or staging content in a buffer. Here's an example of the whole-file-at-once approach:

file-system/read-simple.js

```
const fs = require('fs');
fs.readFile('target.txt', function (err, data) {
  if (err) {
    throw err;
  }
  console.log(data.toString());
});
```

Save this file as read-simple.js and run it as usual with node --harmony:

```
$ node --harmony read-simple.js
```

You'll see the contents of target.txt echoed to the command line. If the file is empty, all you'll see is a blank line.

Notice how the first parameter to the readFile() callback handler is err. If readFile() is successful, then err will be false. Otherwise the err parameter will contain an Error object. This is a common error-reporting pattern in Node, especially for built-in modules. In our example's case, we throw the error if there was one. Recall that an uncaught exception in Node will halt the program by escaping the event loop.

The second parameter to our callback, data, is a buffer; the same kind that was passed to our various callbacks in previous sections.

Writing a file using the whole-file approach is similar. Here's an example:

file-system/write-simple.js

```
const fs = require('fs');
fs.writeFile('target.txt', 'a witty message', function (err) {
  if (err) {
    throw err;
  }
  console.log("File saved!");
});
```

This program writes "a witty message" to target.txt (creating it if it doesn't exist, or overwriting it if it does). If for any reason the file couldn't be written, then the err parameter will contain an Error object.

Creating Read and Write Streams

You create a read stream or a write stream by using fs.createReadStream() and fs.createWriteStream(), respectively. For example, here's a very short program called cat.js. It uses a file stream to pipe a file's data to standard output:

file-system/cat.js

```
#!/usr/bin/env node --harmony
require('fs').createReadStream(process.argv[2]).pipe(process.stdout);
```

Because the first line starts with #!, you can execute this program directly in Unix-like systems. It doesn't need to be passed into the node program.

Use chmod to make it executable:

```
$ chmod +x cat.js
```

Then, to run it, send the name of the chosen file as an additional argument:

```
$ ./cat.js <file_name>
```

The code in cat.js does not bother assigning the fs module to a variable. The require() function returns a module object, so we can call methods on it directly.

You can also listen for data events from the file stream instead of calling pipe(). The following program called read-stream.js does this:

file-system/read-stream.js

```
const
  fs = require('fs'),
  stream = fs.createReadStream(process.argv[2]);
stream.on('data', function(chunk) {
  process.stdout.write(chunk);
});
stream.on('error', function(err) {
  process.stderr.write("ERROR: " + err.message + "\n");
});
```

Here we use process.stdout.write() to echo data, rather than console.log(). The incoming data chunks already contain any newline characters from the input file. We don't need the extra line that console.log() would add.

When working with an EventEmitter, the way to handle errors is to listen for error events. Let's trigger an error to see what happens. Run the program, but specify a file that doesn't exist:

```
$ node --harmony read-stream.js no-such-file
ERROR: ENOENT, open 'no-such-file'
```

Since we're listening for error events, Node invokes our handler (and then proceeds to exit normally). If you don't listen for error events, but one happens anyway, Node will throw an exception. And as we saw before, an uncaught exception will cause the process to terminate.

Blocking the Event Loop with Synchronous File Access

The file-access methods we've discussed in this chapter so far are *asynchronous*. They perform their I/O duties—waiting as necessary—completely in the background, only to invoke callbacks later. This is by far the preferred way to do I/O in Node.

Even so, many of the methods in the fs module have synchronous versions as well. These end in *Sync*, like readFileSync, for example. Doing synchronous file access might look familiar to you if you haven't done a lot of async development in the past. However, it comes at a substantial cost.

When you use the *Sync methods, the Node.js process will *block* until the I/O finishes. This means Node won't execute any other code, won't trigger any callbacks, won't process any events, won't accept any connections—nothing. It'll just sit there indefinitely waiting for the operation to complete.

However, synchronous methods are simpler to use since they lack the callback step. They either return successfully or throw an exception, without the need for a callback function. There actually are cases where this style of access is OK; we'll discuss them in the next section.

Here's an example of how to read a file using the readFileSync() method:

```
const
  fs = require('fs'),
  data = fs.readFileSync('target.txt');
process.stdout.write(data.toString());
```

The return value of readFileSync() is a buffer—the same as the parameter passed to callbacks of the asynchronous readFile() method we saw before.

Performing Other File-System Operations

Node's fs module has many other methods that map nicely onto POSIX conventions. (POSIX is a family of standards for interoperability between operating systems—including file-system utilities.) To name a few examples, you can copy() files and unlink() (delete) them. You can use chmod() to change permissions and mkdir() to create directories.

These functions rely on the same kinds of callback parameters we've used in this chapter. They're all asynchronous by default, but many come with equivalent *Sync versions.

The Two Phases of a Node Program

Given the cost that blocking has on the Node event loop, you might think it's always bad to use synchronous file-access methods. To understand when it's OK, you can think of Node programs as having two phases.

In the initialization phase, the program is getting set up, bringing in libraries, reading configuration parameters, and doing other mission-critical tasks. If something goes wrong at this early stage, not much can be done, and it's best to fail fast. The only time you should consider synchronous file access is during the initialization phase of your program.

The second phase is the operation phase, when the program churns through the event loop. Since many Node programs are networked, this means accepting connections, making requests, and waiting on other kinds of I/O. You should *never* use synchronous file-access methods during this phase.

The require() function is an example of this principle in action—it synchronously evaluates the target module's code and returns the module object. Either the module will successfully load, or the program will fail right away.

As a rule of thumb, if your program couldn't possibly succeed without the file, then it's OK to use synchronous file access. If your program could conceivably continue about its business, then it's better to take the safe route and stick to asynchronous I/O.

Wrapping Up

In this chapter we've used Node to perform file operations in Node's evented, asynchronous, callback-oriented way. You learned how to watch files for changes, and read and write files. You also learned how to spawn child processes and access command-line arguments.

Along the way, we covered the EventEmitter class. We used the on() method to listen for events and handle them in our callback functions. And we used Streams—which are a special kind of EventEmitter—to process data in buffered chunks or pipe it directly to other streams.

Oh, and let's not forget about errors. You learned Node's convention of passing an err argument to callbacks, and how error events can be captured from an EventEmitter.

Keep these patterns in mind as you continue through the book. Third-party libraries sometimes have different styles, but the concepts you've learned here reappear throughout the Node ecosystem.

In the next chapter we'll dig into the other form of server-side I/O: network connections. We'll explore the domain of networked services, building on the concepts and practices developed here.

Here are some bonus questions for you to try out your newly gained Node knowledge.

Fortifying Code

The various example programs we developed in this chapter lack many safety checks. Consider the following questions, and how you'd change the code to address them:

- In the file-watching examples, what happens if the target file doesn't exist?
- What happens if a file being watched gets deleted?

Expanding Functionality

In an early example of our file-watcher program, we pulled the filename to watch from process.argv. Consider these questions:

- Instead, how would you take the *process to spawn* from process.argv?
- How would you pass an arbitrary number of additional parameters from process.argv to the spawned process (e.g., node --harmony watcher-hw.js ls -l -h)?

CHAPTER 3

Networking with Sockets

Node.js is built from the ground up to do networked programming. In this chapter, we'll explore Node's built-in support for low-level socket connections. TCP sockets form the backbone of modern networked applications, and understanding them will serve you well as we do more complex networking through the rest of the book.

As you develop socket-based servers and clients, you'll learn about the following Node.js aspects.

Architecture and Core

The asynchronous programming techniques we explored in the last chapter will be even more important here. You'll learn how to extend Node.js classes like EventEmitter. You'll create custom modules to house reusable code.

Patterns

A network connection has two endpoints. A common pattern is for one endpoint to act as the server while the other is the client. We'll develop both kinds of endpoints in this chapter, as well as a JavaScript Object Notation (JSON)-based protocol for client/server communication.

JavaScriptisms

The JavaScript language has an interesting inheritance model. You'll learn about Node's utilities for creating class-like relationships between objects.

Supporting Code

Testing is important to ensure that our programs behave the way we expect them to. In this chapter, we'll develop a test server that behaves badly on purpose to probe edge cases of our protocol.

To begin, we'll develop a simple and complete TCP server program. Then we'll iteratively improve the server as we address concerns such as robustness, modularity, and testability.

Listening for Socket Connections

Networked services exist to do two things: connect endpoints and transmit information between them. No matter what kind of information is transmitted, a connection must first be made.

In this section, you'll learn how to create socket-based services using Node.js. We'll develop an example application that sends data to connected clients, then we'll connect to this service using standard command-line tools. By the end, you'll have a good idea of how Node does the client/server pattern.

Binding a Server to a TCP Port

TCP socket connections consist of two *endpoints*. One endpoint *binds* to a numbered port while the other endpoint *connects* to a port.

This is a lot like a telephone system. One phone binds a given phone number for a long time. A second phone places a call—it connects to the bound number. Once the call is answered, information (sound) can travel both ways.

In Node.js, the bind and connect operations are provided by the net module. Binding a TCP port to listen for connections looks like this:

```
"use strict";
const
  net = require('net'),
  server = net.createServer(function(connection) {
    // use connection object for data transfer
  });
server.listen(5432);
```

The net.createServer() method takes a callback function and returns a Server object. Node invokes the callback function whenever another endpoint connects. The connection parameter is a Socket object that you can use to send or receive data.

Calling server.listen() binds the specified port. In this case, we're binding TCP port number 5432. Figure 4, *A Node.js server binding a TCP socket for listening,* on page 25 shows this basic setup. The figure shows our one Node.js process whose server binds a TCP port. Any number of clients—which may or may not be Node.js processes—can connect to that bound port.

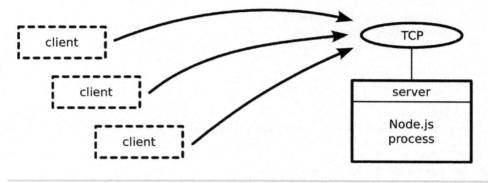

Figure 4—A Node.js server binding a TCP socket for listening

Our server program doesn't do anything with the connection yet. Let's fix that by using it to send some useful information to the client.

Writing Data to a Socket

In Chapter 2, *Wrangling the File System*, on page 9, we developed some simple file utilities that would take action whenever a target file changed. Let's reuse the file changes as a source of information for our example networked service. This will give us something to code against as we dig into aspects of Node.js development.

Open your favorite text editor and enter this:

```
networking/net-watcher.js
'use strict';
const

  fs = require('fs'),
  net = require('net'),

  filename = process.argv[2],

  server = net.createServer(function(connection) {

    // reporting
    console.log('Subscriber connected.');
    connection.write("Now watching '" + filename + "' for changes...\n");

    // watcher setup
    let watcher = fs.watch(filename, function() {
      connection.write("File '" + filename + "' changed: " + Date.now() + "\n");
    });
```

```
    // cleanup
    connection.on('close', function() {
      console.log('Subscriber disconnected.');
      watcher.close();
    });

  });

if (!filename) {
  throw Error('No target filename was specified.');
}

server.listen(5432, function() {
  console.log('Listening for subscribers...');
});
```

Save the file as net-watcher.js. Most of the code here is taken from previous examples in the book, so it should look pretty familiar. The novel parts to the net-watcher program begin inside the callback function given to createServer(). This callback function does three things:

- It reports that the connection has been established (both to the client with connection.write and to the console).

- It begins listening for changes to the target file, saving the returned watcher object. This callback sends change information to the client using connection.write.

- It listens for the connection's close event so it can report that the subscriber has disconnected and stop watching the file, with watcher.close().

Finally, notice the callback passed into server.listen() at the end. Node invokes this function after it has successfully bound port 5432 and is ready to start receiving connections.

Connecting to a TCP Socket Server with Telnet

Now let's run the net-watcher program and confirm that it behaves the way we expect. This will require a little terminal juggling.

To run and test the net-watcher program, you'll need three terminal sessions: one for the service itself, one for the client, and one to trigger changes to the watched file. In the first terminal, run the net-watcher program:

```
$ node --harmony net-watcher.js target.txt
Listening for subscribers...
```

This program creates a service listening on TCP port 5432. To connect to it, open a second terminal and use the telnet program like so:

```
$ telnet localhost 5432
Trying 127.0.0.1...
Connected to localhost.
Escape character is '^]'.
Now watching target.txt for changes...
```

Back in the first terminal, you should see this:

```
Subscriber connected.
```

Finally, to trigger a change to the watched file, open a third terminal and touch the file target.txt:

```
$ touch target.txt
```

In the telnet terminal, after a moment you should see a line like this:

```
File 'target.txt' changed: Sat Jan 12 2013 12:35:52 GMT-0500 (EST)
```

You can kill the telnet session by typing Ctrl-] and then Ctrl-C. If you do, you'll see the following line appear in the first terminal:

```
Subscriber disconnected.
```

To terminate the net-watcher service, type Ctrl-C from its terminal.

The following figure outlines the setup we just created. The net-watcher process (box) binds a TCP port and watches a file—both resources are shown as ovals.

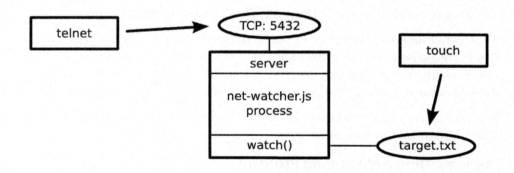

Figure 5—A Node.js program watching a file and reporting changes to connected TCP clients

More than one subscriber can connect and receive updates simultaneously. If you open additional terminals and connect to port 5432 with telnet, they'll all receive updates when you touch the target file.

TCP sockets are useful for communicating between networked computers. But if you need processes on the same computer to communicate, Unix sockets offer a more efficient alternative. The net module can create this kind of socket as well, which we'll look at next.

Listening on Unix Sockets

To see how the net module uses Unix sockets, let's modify the net-watcher program to use this kind of communication channel. Keep in mind that Unix sockets work only on Unix-like environments.

Open the net-watcher.js program and change the server.listen() section to this:

```
server.listen('/tmp/watcher.sock', function() {
  console.log('Listening for subscribers...');
});
```

Save the file as net-watcher-unix.js, then run the program as before:

```
$ node --harmony net-watcher-unix.js target.txt
Listening for subscribers...
```

To connect a client, we now need nc instead of telnet. nc is short for netcat, a TCP/UDP socket utility program that also supports Unix sockets.

```
$ nc -U /tmp/watcher.sock
Now watching target.txt for changes...
```

Unix sockets can be faster than TCP sockets because they don't require invoking network hardware. However, they're local to the machine.

That concludes the basics of creating network socket servers in Node. We discovered how to create socket servers and connect to them using common client utility programs like telnet and nc. This framework will supply the backdrop for the rest of the examples in the chapter.

Next, we'll beef up our service by transforming the data into a parsable format. This will put us in position to develop custom client applications.

Implementing a Messaging Protocol

We've just explored how to create socket servers that listen for incoming connections in Node. So far, our example programs have sent plain-text messages that are meant to be read by a human. In this section, we'll design and implement a better protocol.

A *protocol* is a set of rules that defines how endpoints in a system communicate. Any time you develop a networked application in Node, you're working with one or more protocols. Here we'll create a protocol based on passing JSON encoded messages over TCP.[1]

JSON is incredibly prevalent in Node.js programming and in JavaScript programming generally. We'll use it extensively for data serialization and configuration throughout the book. JSON is significantly easier to program clients against than plain text, and it's still human-readable.

We'll implement client and server endpoints that use our new JSON-based protocol. This will give us opportunities to develop test cases and refactor our code into reusable modules.

Serializing Messages with JSON

Let's develop the message-passing protocol that uses JSON to serialize messages. Each message is a JSON-serialized object, which is a hash of key-value pairs. Here's an example JSON object with two key-value pairs:

```
{"key":"value","anotherKey":"anotherValue"}
```

The net-watcher service we've been developing in this chapter sends two kinds of messages that we need to convert to JSON:

- When the connection is first established, the client receives the string *Now watching target.txt for changes...*

- Whenever the target file changes, the client receives a string like this: *File 'target.txt' changed: Sat Jan 12 2013 12:35:52 GMT-0500 (EST)*

We'll encode the first kind of message this way:

```
{"type":"watching","file":"target.txt"}
```

The type field indicates that this is a watching message—the specified file is now being watched.

The second type of message is encoded this way:

```
{"type":"changed","file":"target.txt","timestamp":1358175733785}
```

Here the type field announces that the target file has changed. The timestamp field contains an integer value representing the number of milliseconds since midnight, January 1, 1970. This happens to be an easy time format to work with in JavaScript. For example, you can get the current time in this format with Date.now().

---

1. http://json.org/

Notice that there are no line breaks in our JSON messages. Although JSON is whitespace agnostic—it ignores whitespace outside of string values—our protocol will use newlines to separate messages. We'll call this protocol Line-Delimited JSON (LDJ).

Switching to JSON Messages

Now that we've defined an improved, computer-accessible protocol, let's modify the net-watcher service to use it. Then we'll create client programs that receive and interpret these messages.

Our task is to use JSON.stringify() to encode message objects and send them out through connection.write(). Open your editor to the net-watcher.js program. Find the following line:

```
connection.write("Now watching '" + filename + "' for changes...\n");
```

And replace it with this:

```
connection.write(JSON.stringify({
  type: 'watching',
  file: filename
}) + '\n');
```

Next, find the call to connection.write() inside the watcher:

```
connection.write("File '" + filename + "' changed: " + Date.now() + "\n");
```

And replace it with this:

```
connection.write(JSON.stringify({
  type: 'changed',
  file: filename,
  timestamp: Date.now()
}) + '\n');
```

Save this updated file as net-watcher-json-service.js. Run the new program with node --harmony as always, remembering to specify a target file. Then connect using telnet from a second terminal:

```
$ telnet localhost 5432
Trying 127.0.0.1...
Connected to localhost.
Escape character is '^]'.
{"type":"watching","file":"target.txt"}
```

When you touch the target.txt file, you'll see output like this from your client:

```
{"type":"changed","file":"target.txt","timestamp":1367038720325}
```

Now we're ready to write a client program that processes these messages.

Creating Socket Client Connections

So far in this chapter, we've explored the server side of Node sockets. Here we'll write a client program in Node to receive JSON messages from our net-watcher-json-service program. We'll start with a naive implementation, and then improve upon it through the rest of the chapter.

Open an editor and insert this:

```
networking/net-watcher-json-client.js
"use strict";
const
  net = require('net'),
  client = net.connect({port: 5432});
client.on('data', function(data) {
  let message = JSON.parse(data);
  if (message.type === 'watching') {
    console.log("Now watching: " + message.file);
  } else if (message.type === 'changed') {
    let date = new Date(message.timestamp);
    console.log("File '" + message.file + "' changed at " + date);
  } else {
    throw Error("Unrecognized message type: " + message.type);
  }
});
```

Save this program as net-watcher-json-client.js.

This short program uses net.connect() to create a client connection to localhost port 5432, then waits for data. The client object is a Socket, just like the incoming connection we saw on the server side.

Whenever a data event happens, our callback function takes the incoming buffer object, parses the JSON message, and then logs an appropriate message to the console.

To run the program, first make sure the net-watcher-json-service is running. Then, in another terminal, run the client:

```
$ node --harmony net-watcher-json-client.js
Now watching: target.txt
```

If you touch the target file, you'll see output like this:

```
File 'target.txt' changed at Mon Jan 14 2013 19:35:14 GMT-0500 (EST)
```

Success! This program works, but it's far from perfect. Consider what happens when the connection ends or if it fails to connect in the first place. This program only listens for data events, not end events or error events. We could listen for these events and take appropriate action when they happen.

But there's actually a deeper problem lurking in our code—caused by assumptions we've made about message boundaries. In the next section we'll develop a test that exposes this bug so we can fix it.

Testing Network Application Functionality

Functional tests assure us that our code does what we expect it to do. In this section, we'll develop a test for our networked file-watching server and client programs. We'll create a mock server that conforms to our LDJ protocol while exposing flaws in the client.

After we write the test, we'll fix the client code so that it passes. This will bring up many Node concepts, include extending core classes, creating and using custom modules, and developing on top of EventEmitters. But first we need to understand a problem lurking in our client/server programs as currently written.

Understanding the Message-Boundary Problem

When you develop networked programs in Node, they'll often communicate by passing messages. In the best case, a message will arrive all at once. But sometimes messages will arrive in pieces, split into distinct data events. To develop networked applications, you'll need to deal with these splits when they happen.

The LDJ protocol we developed earlier separates messages with newline characters. Each newline character is the *boundary* between two messages. Here's an example of a series of messages, with newline characters specifically called out:

```
{"type":"watching","file":"target.txt"}\n
{"type":"changed","file":"target.txt","timestamp":1358175758495}\n
{"type":"changed","file":"target.txt","timestamp":1358175779021}\n
```

Recall the service we've been developing so far in this chapter. Whenever a change happens, it encodes and sends a message to the connection, including the trailing newline. Each line of output corresponds to a single data event in the connected client. Or, to put it another way, the data event boundaries exactly match up with the message boundaries.

Our client program currently relies on this behavior. It parses each message by sending the contents of the data buffer directly into JSON.parse():

```
client.on('data', function(data) {
  let message = JSON.parse(data);
  // ...
});
```

But consider what would happen if a message were split down the middle, and arrived as two separate data events. Such a split could easily happen in the wild, especially for large messages. The following figure shows an example of a split message.

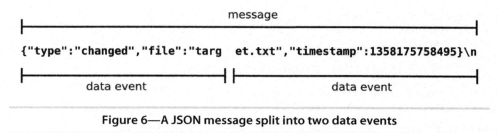

Figure 6—A JSON message split into two data events

Let's create a test service that sends a split message like this one and find out how the client responds.

Implementing a Test Service

Writing robust Node applications means gracefully handling network problems like split inputs, broken connections, and bad data. Here we'll implement a test service that purposefully splits a message into multiple chunks.

Open your editor and enter this:

networking/net-watcher-json-test-service.js
```
"use strict";
const

  net = require('net'),

  server = net.createServer(function(connection) {

    console.log('Subscriber connected');

    // send the first chunk immediately
    connection.write(
      '{"type":"changed","file":"targ'
    );

    // after a one second delay, send the other chunk
    let timer = setTimeout(function(){
      connection.write('et.txt","timestamp":1358175758495}' + "\n");
      connection.end();
    }, 1000);

    // clear timer when the connection ends
    connection.on('end', function(){
```

```
    clearTimeout(timer);
    console.log('Subscriber disconnected');
  });

});

server.listen(5432, function() {
  console.log('Test server listening for subscribers...');
});
```

Save this file as net-watcher-json-test-service.js and run it:

```
$ node --harmony net-watcher-json-test-service.js
Test server listening for subscribers...
```

This test service differs from our previous net-watcher-json-service in a few ways. Rather than setting up a file-system watcher, as we did for the real service, here we just return the first predetermined chunk immediately.

Then we set up a timer to send the second chunk after a one-second delay. The JavaScript function setTimeout() takes two parameters: a function to invoke and an amount of time in milliseconds. After the specified amount of time, the function will be called.

Finally, whenever the connection ends, we use clearTimeout() to unschedule the callback. Unscheduling the callback is necessary since it would fail if it were to execute. After the connection has closed, any calls to connection.write() will trigger error events.

At last, let's find out what happens when we connect with the client program:

```
$ node --harmony net-watcher-json-client.js

undefined:1
{"type":"changed","file":"targ
                              ^
SyntaxError: Unexpected end of input
    at Object.parse (native)
    at Socket.<anonymous> (./net-watcher-json-client.js:10:20)
    at Socket.EventEmitter.emit (events.js:96:17)
    at TCP.onread (net.js:397:14)
```

The error *Unexpected end of input* tells us that the message was not complete and valid JSON. Our client attempted to send half a message to JSON.parse(), which expects only whole, properly formatted JSON strings as input.

At this point, we've successfully simulated the case of a split message coming from the server. Now let's fix the client to work with it.

Extending Core Classes in Custom Modules

The Node program we made in the last section exposed a flaw in our client code; namely, that it doesn't buffer its inputs. Any message that arrives as multiple data events will crash it.

So really the client program has two jobs to do. One is to buffer incoming data into messages. The other is to handle each message when it arrives.

Rather than cramming both of these jobs into one Node program, the right thing to do is to turn at least one of them into a Node *module*. We'll create a module that handles the input-buffering piece so that the main program can reliably get full messages. Along the way, we'll need to talk about custom modules and extending core classes in Node.

Extending EventEmitter

To relieve the client program from the danger of split JSON messages, we'll implement an LDJ buffering client module. Then we'll incorporate it into the network-watcher client.

Inheritance in Node

First let's have a look at how Node does inheritance. The following code sets up LDJClient to inherit from EventEmitter.

```
networking/ldj.js
const
  events = require('events'),
  util = require('util'),
  // client constructor
  LDJClient = function(stream) {
    events.EventEmitter.call(this);
  };
util.inherits(LDJClient, events.EventEmitter);
```

LDJClient is a *constructor function*, which means other code should call new LDJ-Client(stream) to get an instance. The stream parameter is an object that emits data events, such as a Socket connection.

Inside the constructor function, we call the EventEmitter constructor on this. That line of code is roughly equivalent to calling super() in languages with classical inheritance.

Finally, we call util.inherits() to make LDJClient's *prototypal parent* object the EventEmitter *prototype*. If this sounds cryptic to you, don't worry. It's like saying "class LDJClient inherits from EventEmitter" in languages with a classical inheritance model. It means that if you look for a property on an LDJClient and it's not there, the EventEmitter is the next place to look.

There are other ways to do inheritance in JavaScript, but this is how Node.js's own modules are structured. We'll investigate some alternatives in later chapters. But for now, let's follow the Node.js core library style.

Code to use LDJClient might look like this:

```
const client = new LDJClient(networkStream);
client.on('message', function(message) {
  // take action for this message
});
```

Even though the client object doesn't have an on() method directly, its prototypal grandparent, EventEmitter, does.

The inheritance framework is now in place, but we haven't implemented anything to emit message events. Let's look at this next, and talk about buffering data events in Node.

Buffering Data Events

It's time to use the stream parameter in the LDJClient to retrieve and buffer input. The goal is to take the incoming raw data from the stream and convert it into message events containing the parsed message objects.

Take a look at the following updated constructor function. It appends incoming data chunks to a running buffer string and scans for line endings (which should be JSON message boundaries).

```
networking/ldj.js
LDJClient = function(stream) {
  events.EventEmitter.call(this);
  let
    self = this,
    buffer = '';
  stream.on('data', function(data) {
    buffer += data;
    let boundary = buffer.indexOf('\n');
    while (boundary !== -1) {
      let input = buffer.substr(0, boundary);
      buffer = buffer.substr(boundary + 1);
      self.emit('message', JSON.parse(input));
      boundary = buffer.indexOf('\n');
    }
  });
};
```

This constructor function starts out by calling the EventEmitter constructor, just like before. Then we set up the local variable self to capture this.

In JavaScript, the value of this is assigned inside each function when it is invoked, at runtime. The value of this is not tightly bound to any particular object like in classical languages. It's more like a special variable.

Setting a separate variable (self) to the same value guarantees that we're referring to the correct object inside our data event handler. You have to be careful about this in JavaScript, especially when nested functions are involved.

Inside the data event handler, we append raw data to the end of the buffer and then pull completed messages off the front. Each message string is sent through JSON.parse() and finally emitted by the LDJClient as a message event via self.emit(). At this point, the problem we started with (handling split messages) is effectively solved. Whether ten messages come in on a single data event or only half of one does, they'll all precipitate message events on the LDJClient instance.

Next we need to put this class into a Node module so our upstream client can use it.

Exporting Functionality in a Module

Let's pull together the previous code samples and expose LDJClient as a module. Open a text editor and insert the following:

```
networking/ldj.js
"use strict";
const
  events = require('events'),
  util = require('util'),
  // client constructor
  LDJClient = function(stream) {
    events.EventEmitter.call(this);
    let
      self = this,
      buffer = '';
    stream.on('data', function(data) {
      buffer += data;
      let boundary = buffer.indexOf('\n');
      while (boundary !== -1) {
        let input = buffer.substr(0, boundary);
        buffer = buffer.substr(boundary + 1);
        self.emit('message', JSON.parse(input));
        boundary = buffer.indexOf('\n');
      }
    });
  };
```

```
util.inherits(LDJClient, events.EventEmitter);

// expose module methods
exports.LDJClient = LDJClient;
exports.connect = function(stream){
  return new LDJClient(stream);
};
```

Save the file as ldj.js. The code for this module is the combination of previous examples, plus the new exports section at the end.

In a Node module, the exports object is the bridge between the module code and the outside world. Any properties you set on exports will be available to code that pulls in the module.

In our case, we export the LDJClient constructor function and a convenience method called connect(). This method makes it a little easier for upstream code to create an LDJClient instance.

Code to use the LDJ module will look something like this:

```
const
  ldj = require('./ldj.js'),
  client = ldj.connect(networkStream);

client.on('message', function(message) {
  // take action for this message
});
```

Notice that the require() function takes an actual path here, rather than the shorthand module names we've seen previously, like fs, net, and util. When a path is provided to require(), it will attempt to resolve the path relative to the current file.

Our module is done! Finally, let's augment the network-watching client to use the module, bringing it all together.

Importing a Custom Node Module

It's time to make use of our custom module. Let's modify the client to use it rather than reading directly from the stream.

Open a text editor and enter the following:

```
networking/net-watcher-ldj-client.js
"use strict";
const
  net = require('net'),
  ldj = require('./ldj.js'),
```

```
    netClient = net.connect({ port: 5432 }),
    ldjClient = ldj.connect(netClient);

ldjClient.on('message', function(message) {
  if (message.type === 'watching') {
    console.log("Now watching: " + message.file);
  } else if (message.type === 'changed') {
    console.log(
      "File '" + message.file + "' changed at " + new Date(message.timestamp)
    );
  } else {
    throw Error("Unrecognized message type: " + message.type);
  }
});
```

Save this file as net-watcher-ldj-client.js. Note that it's similar to our net-watcher-json-client from *Creating Socket Client Connections*, on page 31. The major difference is that instead of sending data buffers directly to JSON.parse(), this program relies on the ldj module to produce message events.

To make sure it solves the split-message problem, run the test service:

```
$ node --harmony net-watcher-json-test-service.js
Test server listening for subscribers...
```

Then use the new client to connect to it:

```
$ node --harmony net-watcher-ldj-client.js
File 'target.txt' changed at Mon Jan 14 2013 10:02:38 GMT-0500 (EST)
```

Success! You now have a server and client that use a custom message format to communicate. Let's review what we covered before moving on to even bigger things.

Wrapping Up

This chapter explored how to write socket-based networked applications in Node. We developed both ends of a server/client interaction and created a JSON-based protocol for them to communicate.

When our assumptions about the protocol began to fail us, we developed a test case to expose the problem. We saw how to write a custom Node module and how to extend Node core classes, including EventEmitter. We also learned one technique for buffering streamed data and incrementally scanning it for messages.

Writing simple networked applications in Node, like the ones in this chapter, doesn't take very much code. With only a few lines, you can have a functioning server or client application.

However, writing robust applications is harder when you consider all the ways in which a networked application might fail. In the next chapter, we'll use a super-high-performance messaging library to take our Node applications to the next level.

The following bonus questions ask you to improve the code from this chapter, making it more testable, more robust, and more modular.

Testability

The server and client programs we developed in this chapter are somewhat coupled. For example, to test our client-side program we had to develop another server application.

- How could you divide up and expose the functionality to make it more testable?

  Hint: consider how you might separate out functionality into testable modules.

Robustness

The LDJClient developed in this chapter is somewhat fragile. The questions in this section ask you to expand on its implementation in key ways.

- The LDJClient handles the case in which a properly formatted JSON string is split over multiple lines, but what happens if an incoming line is not a properly formatted JSON string?

- What *should* happen in this case?

- What, if any, events should LDJClient emit other than message events?

Separating Concerns

The LDJClient takes care of two separable concerns: splitting incoming data into lines, and parsing lines as JSON. How would you further separate LDJClient into two modules, one for each of these concerns?

Lastly, the net-watcher.js at the beginning of this chapter sets up a new watcher for each connected client. If you had thousands of connected clients, this would mean thousands of watchers. How could you decouple the watching of the file from the notification of the connected clients?

CHAPTER 4

Robust Messaging Services

When you write Node.js programs, you'll often use more than just the core libraries. Node's package manager, npm, offers a rich collection of community-developed modules you can use. In this chapter, you'll learn how to make the most out of third-party modules.

In particular, we're going to explore how to write robust messaging services in Node. We saw the beginnings of networked application development last chapter, and now it's time to take it to the next level. Creating these messaging applications will expose you to the following aspects of Node.js development.

Architecture and Core

Node.js is single-threaded, but you can still take advantage of multiple cores or processors by running more processes. In this chapter, you'll use Node's cluster module to create and manage a pool of Node.js worker processes.

Patterns

The endpoints of a networked application can have many roles, and communicate in many ways. We'll explore powerful messaging patterns like publish/subscribe, request/response, and push/pull. These patterns appear often in networked application design; you'll be a better programmer knowing when and how to apply them.

JavaScriptisms

Functions in JavaScript are variadic. This means they can be called with any number of arguments, whether you planned to receive them or not. The messaging library we'll use takes advantage of this feature to send message data to your callbacks.

Supporting Code

npm is an integral part of the Node ecosystem. You'll learn how to use and manage modules provided through npm. Sometimes modules have external dependencies beyond npm; you'll learn how to build those, too.

To create our robust messaging services, we'll use a cross-platform library called ØMQ (pronounced "Zero-M-Q"). The MQ stands for *message queue*. ØMQ provides high-scalability and low-latency messaging. And with its event-loop-based development model, ØMQ goes with Node.js like peanut butter goes with jelly.

After a brief overview of ØMQ, we'll take it for a spin by making improved versions of some of the applications we developed in previous chapters. Then we'll quickly move on to new messaging patterns. Let's get to it!

Advantages of ØMQ

It's fair to ask why we'd use ØMQ for messaging, as opposed to writing everything ourselves. The answer is that the Node community believes in the Unix philosophy: "do one thing well." The committers keep the Node core small and tight, leaving everything else to the broader base of developers who publish their modules through npm.

Although the Node.js core has great, low-level support for binding and connecting to sockets, it leaves out higher-level messaging patterns. ØMQ's purpose is to expose high-level messaging patterns and take care of many low-level networking concerns for you. Take the following examples:

* ØMQ endpoints automatically reconnect if they become unhitched for any reason—like if there's a hiccup in the network or if a process restarts.

* ØMQ delivers only whole messages, so you don't have to create buffers to deal with chunked data.

* ØMQ's low-overhead protocol takes care of many routing details, like sending responses back to the correct clients.

With ØMQ, like with any good library, your application can focus on what really matters. Now, let's get everything set up with npm so we can build fast, robust messaging applications in Node with ØMQ.

Importing External Modules with npm

npm is your gateway to a large and growing pool of open source Node modules. They do everything from stream parsing to connection pooling to session management. You'll rarely write a Node application that doesn't use at least one module from npm. We'll use many external modules in this book, and zmq (the Node binding for ØMQ) is the first.

Modules managed by npm can be pure JavaScript or a combination of Java-Script and native *addon* code.[1] Addons are dynamically linked shared objects—they provide the glue for working with native libraries written in C or C++.

The vast majority of modules can be installed through the npm command-line tool alone, even if they contain addons. But a few, like the zmq module, have additional requirements as well. To use ØMQ with Node, you have to install the ØMQ base library first; then you can pull in the zmq module through npm.

Installing the ØMQ Base Library

Installing the ØMQ library is fairly straightforward on most platforms. Binary and source packages are available from the project download page.[2]

If you're using Mac OS X with Homebrew, you can quickly install ØMQ from the command line.[3]

```
$ brew install zmq
==> Downloading http://download.zeromq.org/zeromq-3.2.3.tar.gz
################################################################## 100.0%
==> Patching
patching file tests/test_disconnect_inproc.cpp
==> ./configure --prefix=/usr/local/Cellar/zeromq/3.2.3
==> make
==> make install
...
==> Summary
 /usr/local/Cellar/zeromq/3.2.3: 54 files, 2.3M, built in 31 seconds
```

To test whether ØMQ was installed successfully, you can try to load its man page with man zmq.

Installing the zmq Node Module

Once you've installed the base ØMQ library, you can use npm to pull down the zmq Node module.

Create a directory called messaging and navigate to this directory on the command line. Then install zmq:

---

1. http://nodejs.org/api/addons.html
2. http://www.zeromq.org/intro:get-the-software
3. http://brew.sh

```
$ npm install zmq
npm http GET https://registry.npmjs.org/zmq
npm http 200 https://registry.npmjs.org/zmq

> zmq@2.4.0 install ./node_modules/zmq
> node-gyp rebuild
  CXX(target) Release/obj.target/zmq/binding.o
  SOLINK_MODULE(target) Release/zmq.node
  SOLINK_MODULE(target) Release/zmq.node: Finished
zmq@2.4.0 node_modules/zmq
```

Notice the call to node-gyp about halfway though. node-gyp is a cross-platform tool for compiling native addons. If anything went wrong with the build, the output should tell you.

When you run the preceding command, npm will download the zmq module to a folder called node_modules under the current directory. To test that the module was installed successfully, run this command:

```
$ node --harmony -p -e 'require("zmq")'
```

The -e flag tells Node to evaluate the provided string, and the -p flag tells it to print that output to the terminal.

If you see a bunch of details about the zmq module fly by, then you're all set. If you see an exception being thrown, then you'll need to stop and troubleshoot.

Now that the library and the Node module are installed, it's time to start programming Node.js with ØMQ!

Message-Publishing and -Subscribing

ØMQ supports a number of different message-passing patterns that work great in Node. We'll start with the publish/subscribe pattern (PUB/SUB).

Recall the code we wrote in Chapter 3, *Networking with Sockets*, on page 23, when we developed a networked file-watching service and a client to connect to it. They communicated over TCP by sending Line-Delimited JavaScript Object Notation (JSON) messages. The server would *publish* information in this format, and any number of client programs could *subscribe* to it.

We had to work hard to make our client code safely handle the message-boundary problem. We created a separate module dedicated to buffering chunked data and emitting messages. Even so, we were left with questions like how to handle network interrupts or server restarts.

ØMQ makes all of this simpler by taking care of low-level details like buffering and reconnecting. Let's see how much easier it is by implementing a watcher that uses ØMQ PUB/SUB instead of naked TCP. This will get us used to the ØMQ way of doing things, and set us up to explore other messaging patterns with Node and ØMQ.

Publishing Messages over TCP

First, let's implement the PUB half of a PUB/SUB pair using the zmq module. Open an editor and enter the following:

`messaging/zmq-watcher-pub.js`
```
'use strict';
const
  fs = require('fs'),
  zmq = require('zmq'),

  // create publisher endpoint
  publisher = zmq.socket('pub'),

  filename = process.argv[2];

fs.watch(filename, function(){

  // send message to any subscribers
  publisher.send(JSON.stringify({
    type: 'changed',
    file: filename,
    timestamp: Date.now()
  }));

});

// listen on TCP port 5432
publisher.bind('tcp://*:5432', function(err) {
  console.log('Listening for zmq subscribers...');
});
```

Save the file as zmq-watcher-pub.js. This program is similar to ones we developed in previous chapters, with a few differences.

First, instead of requiring the net module, now we're requiring zmq. We use it to create a publisher endpoint by calling zmq.socket('pub').

Importantly, we have only one call to fs.watch(). Our servers from the last chapter would invoke watch() once for each connected client. Here we have just one file-system watcher, which invokes the publisher's send() method.

Notice that the string we send to publisher.send() is the output of JSON.stringify(). ØMQ does not do any formatting of messages itself—it is only interested in pushing bytes down the wire. It's our job to serialize and deserialize any messages we send through ØMQ.

Finally, we call publisher.bind('tcp://*:5432') to tell ØMQ to listen on TCP port 5432 for subscribers.

Let's get the publisher running:

```
$ node --harmony zmq-watcher-pub.js target.txt
Listening for zmq subscribers...
```

Even though this service uses TCP, we can't simply use telnet to get anything out of it. A ØMQ server requires a ØMQ client because of its high-performance binary protocol.

Now let's implement the subscriber end.

Subscribing to a Publisher

Implementing the SUB portion of the ØMQ PUB/SUB pair requires even less code than the publisher. Open an editor and enter this:

messaging/zmq-watcher-sub.js
```
"use strict";
const
  zmq = require('zmq'),

  // create subscriber endpoint
  subscriber = zmq.socket('sub');

// subscribe to all messages
subscriber.subscribe("");

// handle messages from publisher
subscriber.on("message", function(data) {
  let
    message = JSON.parse(data),
    date = new Date(message.timestamp);
  console.log("File '" + message.file + "' changed at " + date);
});

// connect to publisher
subscriber.connect("tcp://localhost:5432");
```

Save this file as zmq-watcher-sub.js. It uses zmq.socket('sub') to make a subscriber endpoint.

Calling subscriber.subscribe("") tells ØMQ that we want to receive all messages. If you only want certain messages, you can provide a string that acts as a prefix filter. You must call subscribe() at some point in your code—you won't receive any messages until you do.

The subscriber object inherits from EventEmitter. It emits a message event whenever it receives one from a publisher, so we use subscriber.on() to listen for them.

Lastly, we use subscriber.connect() to establish the client end of the connection.

Let's see how these pieces fit together. With the PUB program still running in one terminal, fire up zmq-watcher-sub in a second one:

```
$ node --harmony zmq-watcher-sub.js
```

Then, in a third terminal, touch the target file:

```
$ touch target.txt
```

In the subscriber terminal, you should see output something like this:

```
File 'target.txt' changed at Wed May 22 2013 21:34:10 GMT-0400 (EDT)
```

So far, things look pretty great. The publisher and subscriber programs are able to successfully communicate over the PUB/SUB socket pair.

But it gets even better. Keep those services running; next we'll cover how ØMQ handles network interruptions.

Automatically Reconnecting Endpoints

Let's see what happens when one of the endpoints gets disconnected unexpectedly. Try killing the publisher in its terminal via Ctrl-C.

Afterwards, switch over to the subscriber terminal. You may notice that something strange happened—nothing. The subscriber keeps waiting for messages even though the publisher is down, like nothing happened.

Start up the publisher again in the first terminal, then touch the target file. The subscriber should log a *File changed* message to the console. It's as though they were connected the whole time.

From ØMQ's perspective, it doesn't matter which endpoint starts up first. And it automatically reestablishes the connection when an endpoint comes back online. These characteristics add up to a robust platform that gives you stability without a lot of work on your part.

In our previous examples, both the PUB and SUB endpoints were made from zmq.socket(). This means they both have the power to either bind() or connect().

Our code had the publisher bind a TCP socket (as the server) and the subscriber connect (as the client), but ØMQ doesn't force you to do it this way. We could have flipped it around and had the subscriber bind a socket to which the publisher connects.

When you design a networked application, you'll typically have the stable parts of your architecture bind and have the transient parts connect to them. With ØMQ, you get to decide which parts of your system will be stable, and you get to decide which messaging pattern best suits your needs. But you don't have to decide them at the same time, and it's easy to change your mind later. ØMQ provides flexible, durable pipes for constructing distributed applications.

Like Node.js, ØMQ doesn't have a data-center scaling strategy out of the box. But both provide you with building blocks to get you there.

Next we'll look at a different messaging pattern: request/response. Then we'll tie this in with Node's clustering support to manage a pool of worker processes.

Responding to Requests

The REQ/REP (request/reply) pattern is quite common in networked programming, particularly in Node. We'll use this pattern often in the next couple of chapters, and ØMQ has great support for it. As you'll see in a minute, this is where the "Q" of ØMQ becomes apparent.

In ØMQ, a REQ/REP pair communicates in lockstep. A request comes in, then a reply goes out. Additional incoming requests are *queued* and later dispatched by ØMQ. Your application, however, is only aware of one request at a time.

Let's see how this works, again using the file system as a source of information for building a service. In this scenario, a responder waits for a request for file data, then serves up the content when asked. We'll start with the responder —the REP (reply) part of the REQ/REP pair.

Implementing a Responder

Open an editor and enter the following:

```
messaging/zmq-filer-rep.js
'use strict';
const
  fs = require('fs'),
  zmq = require('zmq'),
  // socket to reply to client requests
  responder = zmq.socket('rep');
```

```
// handle incoming requests
responder.on('message', function(data) {

  // parse incoming message
  let request = JSON.parse(data);
  console.log('Received request to get: ' + request.path);

  // read file and reply with content
  fs.readFile(request.path, function(err, content) {
    console.log('Sending response content');
    responder.send(JSON.stringify({
      content: content.toString(),
      timestamp: Date.now(),
      pid: process.pid
    }));
  });

});

// listen on TCP port 5433
responder.bind('tcp://127.0.0.1:5433', function(err) {
  console.log('Listening for zmq requesters...');
});

// close the responder when the Node process ends
process.on('SIGINT', function() {
  console.log('Shutting down...');
  responder.close();
});
```

Save the file as zmq-filer-rep.js. The program creates a ØMQ REP and uses it to respond to incoming requests.

When a message event happens, we parse out the request from the raw data. Next we call fs.readFile() to asynchronously retrieve the requested file's content. When it arrives, we use the responder's send() method to reply with a JSON serialized response, including the file content and a timestamp. We also include the process ID (pid) of the Node process in the response.

The responder binds to TCP port 5433 of the loopback interface (IP 127.0.0.1) to wait for connections. This makes the responder the stable endpoint of the REP/REQ pair.

Finally, we listen for SIGINT events on the Node process. This Unix signal indicates that the process has received an interrupt signal from the user—typically invoked by pressing Ctrl - C in the terminal. The clean thing to do in this case is ask the responder to gracefully close any outstanding connections.

Start the program in a terminal as usual with node --harmony:

```
$ node --harmony zmq-filer-rep.js
Listening for zmq requesters...
```

Looks like our responder is ready! But to connect to it, we'll need to develop a client, so let's put one together.

Issuing Requests

Creating a requester to work with our responder is pretty short. Open an editor and enter this:

```
messaging/zmq-filer-req.js
"use strict";
const
  zmq = require('zmq'),
  filename = process.argv[2],
  // create request endpoint
  requester = zmq.socket('req');
// handle replies from responder
requester.on("message", function(data) {
  let response = JSON.parse(data);
  console.log("Received response:", response);
});
requester.connect("tcp://localhost:5433");
// send request for content
console.log('Sending request for ' + filename);
requester.send(JSON.stringify({
  path: filename
}));
```

Save the file as zmq-filer-req.js.

This program starts off by creating a ØMQ REQ socket. Then we listen for incoming message events and interpret the data as a JSON serialized response (which we log to the console). The end of the program kicks off the request by connecting to REP socket over TCP and finally calling requester.send(). The JSON request message contains the requested file's path as specified on the command line.

Let's see how these REQ and REP sockets work together. With the zmq-filer-rep program still running in one terminal, run this command in another:

```
$ node --harmony zmq-filer-req.js target.txt
Sending request for target.txt
Received response:  { content: '', timestamp: 1370271311810, pid: 32730 }
```

Success! The REP endpoint received the request, processed it, and sent back a response.

Trading Synchronicity for Scale

There is a catch to using ØMQ REP/REQ socket pairs with Node. Each end-point of the application operates on only one request or one response at a time. There is no parallelism.

We can see this in action by making a small change to the requester program. Open the zmq-filer-req.js file from last section. Find the code that sends the request and wrap it in a for loop like this:

```
for (let i=1; i<=3; i++) {
  console.log('Sending request ' + i + ' for ' + filename);
  requester.send(JSON.stringify({
    path: filename
  }));
}
```

Save this file as zmq-filer-req-loop.js. With the responder still running, invoke the new script using node --harmony:

```
$ node --harmony zmq-filer-req-loop.js target.txt
Sending request 1 for target.txt
Sending request 2 for target.txt
Sending request 3 for target.txt
Received response: { content: '', timestamp: 1370301866142, pid: 35925 }
Received response: { content: '', timestamp: 1370301866144, pid: 35925 }
Received response: { content: '', timestamp: 1370301866147, pid: 35925 }
```

We see that the loop queued three requests, and then we received three responses. This shouldn't be too surprising, but let's take a look at the responder window:

```
$ node --harmony zmq-filer-rep.js
Listening for zmq requesters...
Received request to get: target.txt
Sending response content
Received request to get: target.txt
Sending response content
Received request to get: target.txt
Sending response content
```

The responder program sent a response to each request before even becoming aware of the next queued request. This means Node's event loop was left spinning while the fs.readFile() for each request was being processed.

For this reason, a simple REQ/REP pair is probably not going to suit your high-performance Node.js needs. Next we'll construct a cluster of Node processes using more advanced ØMQ socket types to scale up our throughput.

Routing and Dealing Messages

The REQ/REP socket pair we explored makes request/reply logic easy to code by operating sequentially. A given requester or responder will only ever be aware of one message at a time. For parallel message processing, ØMQ includes the more advanced socket types ROUTER and DEALER. Let's explore these a bit; then we'll be ready to construct our Node.js cluster.

Routing Messages

You can think of a ROUTER socket as a parallel REP socket. Rather than replying to only one message at a time, a ROUTER socket can handle many requests simultaneously. It remembers which connection each request came from and will route reply messages accordingly.

Recall from *Implementing a Messaging Protocol*, on page 28, that any time you do networked programming, you're working with one or more protocols. ØMQ uses the ZeroMQ Message Transport Protocol for exchanging messages.[4] This protocol uses a sequence of low-overhead *frames* to compose messages. A ROUTER socket uses these frames to route each reply message back to the connection that issued the request.

Most of the time your Node programs can ignore the underlying details of ØMQ frames because the simpler socket types only need one frame per message. But the ROUTER socket type uses multiple frames.

Here's an example of how to create a ROUTER socket in Node, with a message handler that grabs all the incoming frames.

```
const
  zmq = require('zmq'),
  router = zmq.socket('router');

router.on('message', function() {
  let frames = Array.prototype.slice.call(null, arguments);

  // ...
});
```

Previously, our message handlers would take a data parameter, but notice how this handler function doesn't take any. The zmq module actually passes all the frames for a message to the handler as arguments to the handler function. It can do this because JavaScript functions are *variadic*—they can receive any number of arguments when called.

---

4. http://rfc.zeromq.org/spec:15

The arguments object inside a function is an array-like object that contains all the arguments that were passed in. Using Array.prototype.slice.call(null, arguments) returns a real JavaScript Array instance with the same contents.

Now that we can get all the frames, let's look at the DEALER socket type.

Dealing Messages

If a ROUTER socket is a parallel REP socket, then a DEALER is a parallel REQ. A DEALER socket can send multiple requests in parallel.

Let's see how a dealer and router work together in Node. Take a look at this code sample:

```
const
  zmq = require('zmq'),
  router = zmq.socket('router'),
  dealer = zmq.socket('dealer');

router.on('message', function() {
  let frames = Array.prototype.slice.call(null, arguments);
  dealer.send(frames);
});
dealer.on('message', function() {
  let frames = Array.prototype.slice.call(null, arguments);
  router.send(frames);
});
```

Here we create both a ROUTER socket and a DEALER socket. Whenever either receives a message, it strips out the frames and sends them to the other socket.

This means incoming requests to the router will be passed off to the dealer to send out to its connections. Likewise, incoming replies to the dealer will be forwarded back to the router, which directs each reply back to the connection that requested it.

The code sample doesn't include any calls to bind() or connect(), so it's not a functional example yet. Even so, you can see the basic structure we're after in Figure 7, *A Node.js program using both ROUTER and DEALER ØMQ sockets*, on page 54.

The box in the center of the figure is the Node program. An incoming REQ socket connects to the ROUTER. When it issues a request message, the ROUTER bounces it over to the DEALER. The DEALER then picks one of the REP sockets connected to it to forward the request.

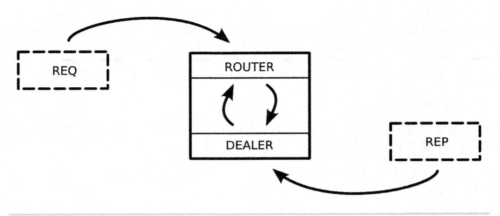

Figure 7—A Node.js program using both ROUTER and DEALER ØMQ sockets

When the REP connection produces a reply, it follows the reverse route. The DEALER receives the reply and bounces it back to the ROUTER. The ROUTER looks at the message's frames to determine its origin and sends the reply back to the connected REQ that sent the initial request.

From the perspective of the REQ and REP sockets, nothing has changed. Each still operates in lockstep, handling one message at a time from the application's perspective. Meanwhile, the ROUTER/DEALER pair can load-balance among the REQ and REP sockets connected on both ends.

Now it's time to put these new socket types to use. Next we'll develop a clustered Node.js application on top of the REQ, REP, ROUTER, and DEALER sockets we've just explored.

Clustering Node.js Processes

In multithreaded systems, doing more work in parallel means spinning up more threads. But Node.js uses a single-threaded event loop, so to take advantage of multiple cores or multiple processors on the same computer, you have to spin up more Node processes.

This is called *clustering* and it's what Node's built-in cluster module does. Clustering is a useful technique for scaling up your Node application when there's unused CPU capacity available. Scaling a Node application is a big topic with lots of choices based on your particular scenario, but no matter how you end up doing it, you'll probably start with clustering.

To explore how the cluster module works, we'll build up a program that manages a pool of worker processes to respond to ØMQ requests. This will be a drop-in replacement for our previous responder program. It will use ROUTER, DEALER, and REP sockets to distribute requests to workers.

In all, we'll end up with a short and powerful program that combines cluster-based, multiprocess work distribution and load-balanced message-passing to boot.

Forking Worker Processes in a Cluster

Back in *Spawning a Child Process*, on page 13, we used the child_process module's spawn() function to fire up a process. This works great for executing non-Node processes from your Node program. But for spinning up copies of the same Node program, forking is a better option.

Each time you call the cluster module's fork() method, it creates a worker process running the same script as the original. To see what I mean, take a look at the following code snippet. It shows the basic framework for a clustered Node application.

```
const cluster = require('cluster');

if (cluster.isMaster) {
  // fork some worker processes
  for (let i = 0; i < 10; i++) {
    cluster.fork();
  }

} else {
  // this is a worker process, do some work
}
```

First, we check whether the current process is the *master* process. If so, we use cluster.fork() to create additional processes. The fork method launches a new Node.js process running the same script, but for which cluster.isMaster is false.

The forked processes are called *workers*. They can intercommunicate with the master process through various events.

For example, the master can listen for workers coming online with code like this:

```
cluster.on('online', function(worker) {
  console.log('Worker ' + worker.process.pid + ' is online.');
});
```

When the cluster module emits an online event, a worker parameter is passed along. One of the properties on this object is process—the same sort of process that you'd find in any Node.js program.

Similarly, the master can listen for processes exiting:

```
cluster.on('exit', function(worker, code, signal) {
  console.log('Worker ' + worker.process.pid + ' exited with code ' + code);
});
```

Like online, the exit event includes a worker object. The event also includes the exit code of the process and what operating-system signal (like SIGINT or SIGTERM) was used to halt the process.

Building a Cluster

Now it's time to put everything together, harnessing Node clustering and the ØMQ messaging patterns we've been talking about. We'll build a program that distributes requests to a pool of worker processes.

Our master Node process will create ROUTER and DEALER sockets and spin up the workers. Each worker will create a REP socket that connects back to the DEALER.

The following figure illustrates how all these pieces fit together. As in previous figures, the rectangles represent Node.js processes. The ovals are the resources bound by ØMQ sockets, and the arrows show which sockets connect to which endpoints.

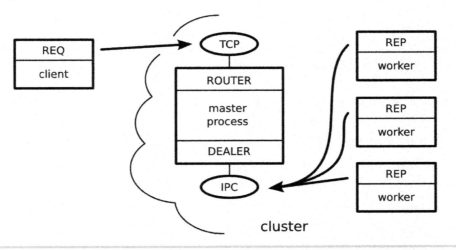

Figure 8—A Node.js cluster that routes requests to a pool of workers

The master process is the most stable part of the architecture (it manages the workers), so it's responsible for doing the binding. The cluster's worker processes and clients of the service all connect to endpoints bound by the master process. Remember that the flow of messages is decided by the socket *types*, not which socket happens to bind or connect.

Now let's get to the code. Open your favorite editor and enter the following.

messaging/zmq-filer-rep-cluster.js

```
Line 1  'use strict';
     -  const
     -    cluster = require('cluster'),
     -    fs = require('fs'),
     5    zmq = require('zmq');
     -
     -  if (cluster.isMaster) {
     -
     -    // master process - create ROUTER and DEALER sockets, bind endpoints
    10    let
     -      router = zmq.socket('router').bind('tcp://127.0.0.1:5433'),
     -      dealer = zmq.socket('dealer').bind('ipc://filer-dealer.ipc');
     -
     -    // forward messages between router and dealer
    15    router.on('message', function() {
     -      let frames = Array.prototype.slice.call(arguments);
     -      dealer.send(frames);
     -    });
     -
    20    dealer.on('message', function() {
     -      let frames = Array.prototype.slice.call(null, arguments);
     -      router.send(frames);
     -    });
     -
    25    // listen for workers to come online
     -    cluster.on('online', function(worker) {
     -      console.log('Worker ' + worker.process.pid + ' is online.');
     -    });
     -
    30    // fork three worker processes
     -    for (let i = 0; i < 3; i++) {
     -      cluster.fork();
     -    }
     -
    35  } else {
     -
     -    // worker process - create REP socket, connect to DEALER
     -    let responder = zmq.socket('rep').connect('ipc://filer-dealer.ipc');
     -
    40    responder.on('message', function(data) {
     -
     -      // parse incoming message
     -      let request = JSON.parse(data);
     -      console.log(process.pid + ' received request for: ' + request.path);
    45
```

```
      // read file and reply with content
      fs.readFile(request.path, function(err, data) {
        console.log(process.pid + ' sending response');
        responder.send(JSON.stringify({
50        pid: process.pid,
          data: data.toString(),
          timestamp: Date.now()
        }));
      });

55
    });

  }
```

Save this file as zmq-filer-rep-cluster.js. This program is a little longer than our previous Node programs, but it should look familiar to you since it's based entirely on snippets we've already discussed.

Notice that the ROUTER listens for incoming TCP connections on port 5433 on line 11. This allows the cluster to act as a drop-in replacement for the zmq-filer-rep.js program we developed earlier.

On line 12, the DEALER socket binds an interprocess connection (IPC) end-point. This is backed by a Unix socket like the one we used in *Listening on Unix Sockets*, on page 28.

By convention, ØMQ IPC files should end in the file extension .ipc. In this case, the filer-dealer.ipc file will be created in the current working directory that the cluster was launched from (if it doesn't exist already).

Let's run the cluster program to see how it works:

```
$ node --harmony zmq-filer-rep-cluster.js
Worker 37174 is online.
Worker 37172 is online.
Worker 37173 is online.
```

So far so good—the master process spun up the workers, and they've all reported in. In a second terminal, fire up our REQ loop program (zmq-filer-req-loop.js):

```
$ node --harmony zmq-filer-req-loop.js
Sending request 1 for target.txt
Sending request 2 for target.txt
Sending request 3 for target.txt
Received response: { pid: 37174, data: '', timestamp: 1371652913066 }
Received response: { pid: 37172, data: '', timestamp: 1371652913075 }
Received response: { pid: 37173, data: '', timestamp: 1371652913083 }
```

Just like our earlier reply program, this clustered approach answers each request in turn.

But notice that the reported process ID (pid) is different for each response received. This shows that the master process is indeed load-balancing the requests to different workers.

Now you have the tools to build a Node.js cluster. There are a few more benefits to using the cluster module for managing worker processes. We'll come to those in Chapter 6, *Scalable Web Services*, on page 87.

Up next, we'll examine one more messaging pattern offered by ØMQ before closing out the chapter.

Pushing and Pulling Messages

So far we've worked with two major message-passing patterns; first we looked at publish/subscribe, then request/reply. There's one more pattern offered by ØMQ that's sometimes good to use with Node.js—PUSH/PULL.

Pushing Jobs to Workers

The PUSH and PULL socket types are useful when you have a queue of jobs that you want to fairly assign among a pool of available workers.

Recall that with a PUB/SUB pair, each subscriber will receive all messages sent by the publisher. In a PUSH/PULL setup, only one puller will receive each message sent by the pusher.

So PUSH will round-robin-distribute messages to connected sockets, just like the DEALER. But unlike the DEALER/ROUTER flow, there is no backchannel. A message traveling from a PUSH socket to a PULL socket is one-way; the puller can't send a response back through the same socket.

Here's a quick example showing how to set up a PUSH socket and distribute 100 jobs. Note that the example is incomplete—it doesn't call bind() or connect() —but it does demonstrate the concept.

```
const
  zmq = require('zmq'),
  pusher = zmq.socket('push');

// wait until pullers are connected and ready, then send 100 jobs ...
for (let i = 0; i < 100; i++) {
  pusher.send(JSON.stringify({
    details: "details about this job."
  });
}
```

And here's an associated PULL socket.

```
const
  zmq = require('zmq'),
  puller = zmq.socket('pull');

// connect to the pusher, announce readiness to work, then wait for work ...

puller.on('message', function(data) {
  let job = JSON.parse(data.toString());

  // do the work described in the job
});
```

Like with ØMQ sockets, either end of a PUSH/PULL pair can bind or connect —the choice comes down to which is the stable part of the architecture.

Using the PUSH/PULL pattern in Node brings up a couple of potential pitfalls hidden in these simple examples. Let's explore them, and what to do to avoid them.

Avoiding Common Pitfalls

The two common pitfalls you're likely to encounter with the PUSH/PULL pattern in Node.js are the first-joiner problem and the limited-resource problem.

The First-Joiner Problem

The *first-joiner problem* is the result of ØMQ being so fast at sending messages and Node.js being so fast at accepting them. Since it takes time to establish a connection, the first puller to successfully connect will pull many or all of the available messages before the second joiner even has a chance to get into the rotation.

To fix this problem, the pusher needs to wait until all of the pullers are ready to receive messages before pushing any. Let's consider a real-world scenario and how we'd solve it.

Say you have a Node cluster, and the master process plans to PUSH a bunch of jobs to three worker processes. Before the master can start pushing, the workers need a way to signal back to the master that they're ready to start pulling jobs. They also need a way to communicate the results of the jobs that they'll eventually complete.

Figure 9, *A Node.js cluster that pushes work to a pool of workers*, on page 61 shows this scenario.

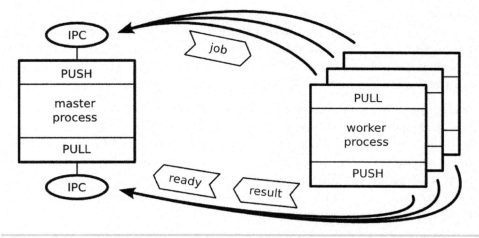

Figure 9—A Node.js cluster that pushes work to a pool of workers

As in previous diagrams, rectangles are Node processes, ovals are resources, and heavy arrows point in the direction the connection is established. The job, ready, and result messages are shown as light arrow boxes pointing in the direction they are sent.

In the top half of the figure, we have the main communication channel—the master's PUSH socket hooked up to the workers' PULL sockets. This is how jobs will be sent to workers.

In the bottom half of the figure, we have a backchannel. This time the master has a PULL socket connected to each worker's PUSH sockets. The workers can PUSH messages like their readiness to work or job results back to the master.

The master process is the stable part of the architecture, so it binds while the workers connect. Since all of the processes are local to the same machine, it makes sense to use IPC for the transport.

The bonus challenge in *Bidirectional Messaging*, on page 63, will ask you to implement the PUSH/PULL cluster described earlier. Note, however, that this is just one solution to the first-joiner problem. You could choose to use a different messaging pattern for the backchannel, like request/reply.

The Limited-Resource Problem

The other common pitfall is the *limited-resource problem*. Node.js is at the mercy of the operating system with respect to the number of resources it can access at the same time. In Unix-speak, these are called *file descriptors*.

Whenever your Node program opens a file or a TCP connection, it uses one of its available file descriptors. When there are none left, Node will start failing to connect to resources when asked. This is an extremely common problem for Node.js developers. I have yet to meet a Node developer who hasn't grappled with the limited-resource problem at one time or another.

Strictly speaking, this problem isn't limited to the PUSH/PULL scenario, but it's very likely to happen there, and here's why. Since Node.js is asynchronous, the puller process can start working on many jobs simultaneously. Every time a message event comes in, the Node process invokes the handler and starts working on the job. If these jobs require accessing system resources —and they almost certainly will—you're liable to exhaust the pool of available file descriptors. Then jobs will quickly start failing.

We'll explore this topic and its solutions in more detail in Chapter 5, *Accessing Databases*, on page 65, when we limit the number of concurrent database connections through a technique called connection pooling.

Wrapping Up

This chapter brought us out of the Node.js core and into the larger world of npm. We discussed how to install and use third-party modules with binary components. In particular, we covered how to use ØMQ.

ØMQ supports a number of message-passing patterns; we got to know several of them. We saw how ØMQ does the publish/subscribe pattern, the request/ reply pattern, and the PUSH/PULL pattern. These patterns are now tools at your disposal for designing networked applications in Node.js, even if you choose not to use the ØMQ library itself.

We also explored Node's clustering capabilities. Using features of Node's cluster module, we spun up a number of worker processes and distributed requests to them. We'll use these capabilities again in Chapter 6, *Scalable Web Services*, on page 87.

The following bonus questions ask you to modify and create new Node.js and ØMQ programs using what you learned from the chapter.

In the next chapter, we'll cover how to use Node to interact asynchronously with several popular databases.

Error Handling

The zmq-filer-rep.js program we created uses fs.readFile() to serve up file contents. However, it doesn't handle the error case.

- What should the program do in the case of an error?

- How would you change the protocol to support sending an error to the requester?

Later in this same program, we listen for the Unix signal SIGINT to detect the user's Ctrl-C in the terminal.

- What happens if the program ends in some other way, like SIGTERM (the termination signal)?

- What happens if there's an unhandled Node.js exception?

  Hint: you can listen for the uncaughtException event on the process object.

Robustness

In *Building a Cluster*, on page 56, we created a Node.js cluster that spins up three worker processes. In the master process, we listened for online events and logged a message when the workers came up. But we didn't specify what should happen when a worker process ends.

- What happens when you kill a worker process from the command line?

  Hint: use kill [pid] from the command line, where [pid] is the worker's process ID.

- How would you change the zmq-filer-rep-cluster.js program to fork a new worker whenever one dies?

Bidirectional Messaging

For this project, you'll need to use ØMQ PUSH/PULL sockets and the Node.js clustering techniques you learned in this chapter. Your clustered program will spin up a pool of three workers and distribute thirty jobs between them. Although this seems like a lot to do, the whole program should be less than 100 lines of code.

Create a Node.js program that uses the cluster and zmq modules and does the following.

The master process should

- Create a PUSH socket and bind it to an IPC endpoint—this socket will be for sending jobs to the workers.

- Create a PULL socket and bind to a different IPC endpoint—this socket will receive messages from workers.

- Keep a count of ready workers (initialized to 0).
- Listen for messages on the PULL socket, and
    - If the message is a ready message, increment the ready counter, or
    - If the message is a result message, output it to the console.
- Spin up three worker processes.
- When the ready counter reaches 3, send thirty job messages out through the PUSH socket.

Each worker process should

- Create a PULL socket and connect it to the master's PUSH endpoint.
- Create a PUSH socket and connect it to the master's PULL endpoint.
- Listen for messages on the PULL socket, and
    - Treat this as a job and respond by sending a result message out on the PUSH socket.
- Send a ready message out on the PUSH socket.

Result messages should include at least the process ID of the worker. This way you can inspect the console output and confirm that the workload is being balanced among the worker processes.

If you get completely stuck, consult the working example available in the downloadable code that accompanies this book. You can do it. Good luck!

CHAPTER 5

Accessing Databases

Data must persist, and databases are a great way to make that happen. As we've seen, Node.js does network I/O asynchronously, and this certainly includes interacting with databases. No matter which database you choose, you'll have to become comfortable making asynchronous requests to it.

Working with databases will offer a convenient context for exploring the following aspects of Node development.

Architecture and Core
> Node.js is fast—really fast. It's easy in Node to exhaust system resources or overload other systems it talks to. You'll learn what to do to mitigate these kinds of problems and how to react to them when they happen.

Patterns
> Asynchronous JavaScript programming can become complex when you have many tasks that depend on each other. You'll learn a couple of techniques for executing tasks in batches or in sequence using an npm module called async. You'll also work extensively with RESTful APIs.

JavaScriptisms
> Sometimes JavaScript code gets executed in a different context than where it was originally written. You'll learn how to export JavaScript functions from one environment to another.

Supporting Code
> In previous chapters we've tested our code by running it in different scenarios. Here you'll use common testing tools with npm to code and run unit tests.

Different databases use different protocols for communicating with clients. Some databases use simple text-based commands over TCP, and some have their own binary protocols. Still other databases use Representational State Transfer (REST).

We'll use CouchDB for exploring databases with Node.[1] CouchDB uses REST for everything, from creating databases to reporting the system status to executing mapreduce queries. Using CouchDB to learn about asynchronous database access in Node has several advantages.

Advantages of CouchDB

Interacting with CouchDB is all about making proper HTTP requests. This will give us the opportunity to talk about HTTP and RESTful practices—information that will be handy in Chapter 6, *Scalable Web Services*, on page 87, when we'll implement our own RESTful web services. And the techniques you'll use here apply to other RESTful APIs, like those published by Amazon and Google.

As a bonus, CouchDB speaks JavaScript. Whenever you store data in CouchDB, you send it a JavaScript Object Notation (JSON) *document*. A document is a JSON object with a couple of special attributes that we'll see shortly. Indexing and querying in CouchDB is done with mapreduce views written in JavaScript, also accessible through REST.

Lastly, npm itself uses CouchDB extensively. The metadata about modules in npm is stored and queried in CouchDB. There is significant overlap between the Node.js core developer group and the CouchDB community.

Let's get CouchDB up and running. Then we'll build out a toolkit for working with it. CouchDB is easy to install on many platforms. Binaries are available from the project website, or you can use a package manager. If you're using Mac OS X with Homebrew, you can install CouchDB with the command brew install couchdb.

Once you have CouchDB installed, start it from the command line with the couchdb command.

```
$ couchdb
Apache CouchDB 1.2.1 (LogLevel=info) is starting.
Apache CouchDB has started. Time to relax.
[info] [<0.31.0>] Apache CouchDB has started on http://127.0.0.1:5984/
```

The specific version of CouchDB doesn't matter much for our purposes. We'll focus on using basic, RESTful operations, which haven't changed from version to version.

Throughout this chapter, you'll develop a number of Node scripts and modules. The first thing you'll need to do is set aside a space for them, starting with a package descriptor.

---

1.   https://couchdb.apache.org/

Creating a Package

Create a directory on your machine somewhere called databases. We'll use this directory for all programs, data files, and examples from this chapter. Next, open an editor and enter the following:

```
databases/package.json
{
  "name": "book-tools",
  "version": "0.1.0",
  "description": "Tools for creating an ebook database.",
  "author": "Your Name <you@yoursite.com> (http://yoursite.com/path)"
}
```

Save this file in your project directory as package.json.

In a Node.js project, the package.json file describes many aspects of the project and its dependencies.[2] This short example includes only the basics: the project's name, version, short description, and author. For your own projects, rather than create a package.json file by hand, you can use npm init. This will prompt you for all the important information.

When you install a module through npm, you have the choice of saving it as a dependency in the package.json. You do this with the --save flag. Run the following command from your project directory:

```
$ npm install --save request
```

This will install the request module and record it as a dependency in your package.json. If you take a look at your package.json file again, you'll see that there's now a dependencies section that looks like this:

```
"dependencies": {
  "request": "~2.26.0"
}
```

When you describe your dependencies in a package.json file, npm can install them all for you. This is most useful when distributing your module, or when collaborators work on the same code base. To install all of the dependencies for the current project, just run npm install with no additional arguments.

Next, let's use the freshly installed request module to start making REST requests to CouchDB.

---

2.   https://npmjs.org/doc/json.html

Making RESTful Requests

At its core, REST is a set of principles built on top of HTTP. With REST, each URL path points to a specific *resource*. In other words, URLs are things. This is in direct contrast to many server designs where a given path invokes a script that does something (URLs are actions).

HTTP itself is a request/reply protocol where each request is made to a URL with a particular *method*. The HTTP method for an incoming request determines what kind of action the server should take on the resource indicated in the URL.

Any database you work with will offer at least the four basic operations: create, read, update, and delete (CRUD). RESTful datastores like CouchDB use a different HTTP method (or *verb*) for each operation. You use POST to create, GET to read, PUT to update, and DELETE to (you guessed it) delete records.

REST from the Command Line

Node's built-in http module has functions for making HTTP requests, but the request module makes it much easier. To learn how to use the request module, we'll first put together a command-line interface (CLI) tool for working with CouchDB. We'll use the CLI to set up a CouchDB database initially and try out some REST semantics.

Open your editor and enter this:

databases/dbcli.js
```
#!/usr/bin/env node --harmony
const
  request = require('request'),
  options = {
    method: process.argv[2] || 'GET',
    url: 'http://localhost:5984/' + (process.argv[3] || '')
  };
request(options, function(err, res, body) {
  if (err) {
    throw Error(err);
  } else {
    console.log(res.statusCode, JSON.parse(body));
  }
});
```

Save this file as dbcli.js. Though short, this program lets you do quite a lot with your CouchDB server. First, this script pulls in the request module. Unlike the modules we've seen so far, which were JavaScript Objects, the request module object is actually a function. The main way you use the module it is by calling it.

The request() function takes two arguments: an options object and a callback. The most important options to set are the HTTP method and the URL you plan to hit. In our case, we grab both the method and path information from the command-line arguments, with sensible defaults.

Since our script starts with the #! directive, it can be executed directly. To make the file executable, go to the terminal and run this:

```
$ chmod +x dbcli.js
```

Now it's time to try it out. Assuming your CouchDB server is running, you should see output like the following:

```
$ ./dbcli.js
200 { couchdb: 'Welcome', version: '1.2.1' }
```

When you issue an HTTP GET request to the server's root (/), CouchDB gives you a welcome message.

Using the CLI for CouchDB REST

A *database* in CouchDB is basically a big collection of documents. Each database lives at a URL path one level down from the root. For example, if you had a database called books it would live at /books. Let's see what happens when we try and GET the as-yet-uncreated books database:

```
$ ./dbcli.js GET books
404 { error: 'not_found', reason: 'no_db_file' }
```

Since there is no books database yet, we get an HTTP 404 Not Found status code. To make a database, use the HTTP verb PUT.

```
$ ./dbcli.js PUT books
201 { ok: true }
```

CouchDB returned a 201 Created status code to tell us that it successfully created the database.

The difference between POST and PUT is subtle but important. If you already have the full URL for the RESTful thing you're working on, then you use PUT. Otherwise, you use POST. So if you're updating an existing resource, PUT is always correct, but to create a new resource you use PUT only if you know the full URL to where that resource will be.

In the case of the books database, we know that it will live at /books, so PUT is the correct verb to use.

Now when we GET the books database, CouchDB responds with a 200 OK status code and information about the database:

```
$ ./dbcli.js GET books
200 { db_name: 'books',
  doc_count: 0,
  doc_del_count: 0,
  update_seq: 0,
  purge_seq: 0,
  compact_running: false,
  disk_size: 79,
  data_size: 0,
  instance_start_time: '1376409945081320',
  disk_format_version: 6,
  committed_update_seq: 0 }
```

If you wanted to remove the books database, you'd use the DELETE HTTP verb. Don't do this now, though; we'll need the books database for our next task, importing lots of data using Node.js.

Importing Real Data

Next we'll use the request module to import a whole bunch of data into the books database. As we do so, we'll run into the limited-resource problem we first saw in *The Limited-Resource Problem*, on page 61. This will give us a backdrop for experimenting with asynchronous coding techniques.

First we need to get some data to work with. We'll use the catalog data from Project Gutenberg, a site dedicated to making public-domain works available as free ebooks.[3]

Downloading Project Gutenberg Data

Project Gutenberg produces catalog download bundles that contain Resource Description Framework (RDF) files for each of their 43,000-plus books. (RDF is an XML-based format.) The bz2 version of the catalog file is about 13 MB. Fully extracted, it contains more than 500 MB of RDF files.

To download and extract the rdf-files.tar.bz2, open a terminal to your databases/ project directory and run the following commands.

```
$ curl -O http://www.gutenberg.org/cache/epub/feeds/rdf-files.tar.bz2
$ tar -xvjf rdf-files.tar.bz2
x cache/epub/0/pg0.rdf
x cache/epub/1/pg1.rdf
x cache/epub/10/pg10.rdf
...
x cache/epub/9998/pg9998.rdf
x cache/epub/9999/pg9999.rdf
x cache/epub/999999/pg999999.rdf
```

---

3.   http://www.gutenberg.org

This will create a cache directory that contains all the RDF files. Each RDF file is named after its Project Gutenberg ID and contains the metadata about one book. For example, book number 132 is Lionel Giles's 1910 translation of *The Art of War* by Sunzi.

Here's a stripped-down excerpt from cache/epub/132/pg132.rdf that shows only the fields that we care about.

```
<rdf:RDF>
  <pgterms:ebook rdf:about="ebooks/132">
    <dcterms:subject>
      <rdf:Description>
        <dcam:memberOf rdf:resource="http://purl.org/dc/terms/LCSH"/>
        <rdf:value>Military art and science -- Early works to 1800</rdf:value>
        <rdf:value>War -- Early works to 1800</rdf:value>
      </rdf:Description>
    </dcterms:subject>
    <dcterms:title>The Art of War</dcterms:title>
  </pgterms:ebook>
  <pgterms:agent rdf:about="2009/agents/4349">
    <pgterms:name>Sunzi (6th cent. BC)</pgterms:name>
  </pgterms:agent>
  <pgterms:agent rdf:about="2009/agents/5101">
    <pgterms:name>Giles, Lionel</pgterms:name>
  </pgterms:agent>
</rdf:RDF>
```

The important pieces of information that we'd like to extract are as follows:

- The Gutenberg ID
- The book's title
- The list of authors (agents)
- The list of subjects

Ideally, we'd like to have all of this information formatted as a JSON document suitable for passing in to CouchDB. But to get a nice JSON representation, we'll have to parse the RDF file.

Parsing XML Data with Node

To parse the XML files, we'll use cheerio, a jQuery-like library for working with XML documents in Node.

First, install cheerio through npm and save the dependency:

```
$ npm install --save cheerio
```

Next, inside your databases project, make a lib directory. We'll create our RDF parsing utility as a module.

Then, open an editor and enter this:

```
databases/lib/rdf-parser.js
Line 1  'use strict';
   -    const
   -      fs = require('fs'),
   -      cheerio = require('cheerio');
   5
   -    module.exports = function(filename, callback) {
   -      fs.readFile(filename, function(err, data){
   -        if (err) { return callback(err); }
   -        let
  10          $ = cheerio.load(data.toString()),
   -          collect = function(index, elem) {
   -            return $(elem).text();
   -          };
  15        callback(null, {
   -          _id: $('pgterms\\:ebook').attr('rdf:about').replace('ebooks/', ''),
   -          title: $('dcterms\\:title').text(),
   -          authors: $('pgterms\\:agent pgterms\\:name').map(collect),
   -          subjects: $('[rdf\\:resource$="/LCSH"] ~ rdf\\:value').map(collect)
  20        });
   -      });
   -    };
```

Save the file as lib/rdf-parser.js.

Like the request module we used earlier, this module sets its exports to a function. Users of the module will call this function, passing in a path to a file and a callback to invoke with the extracted data.

The main module function reads the specified file asynchronously, then loads the data into cheerio. Cheerio gives back an object we assign to the $ variable. This object works much like the jQuery global function $—it provides methods for querying and modifying elements.

The collect() function is a utility method for extracting an array of text nodes from a set of element nodes. The bulk of the logic for this module is encapsulated in the four lines inside the callback() invocation:

- First up, in line 16, we look for the <pgterms:ebook> tag, read its rdf:about= attribute, and pull out just the numerical portion.

- In line 17, we grab the text content of the <dcterms:title> tag.

- In line 18, we find all the <pgterms:name> elements under a <pgterms:agent> and collect their text contents in an array.

- Lastly, in line 19, we use the sibling operator (~) to find the <rdf:value> elements that are siblings of any element whose rdf:resource= attribute ends in *LCSH*, and collect their text contents.

LCSH stands for Library of Congress Subject Headings.[4] They are a collection of indexing terms for use in bibliographic records. We'll use these later to find books on a given subject.

This code is a little dense, but fortunately it doesn't have side effects. That is, this code selects data from a complex schema and reformats it into a simple JavaScript object. Not bad for four lines of code!

OK, so how do we find out if it worked? One way is to write a one-liner and see that it outputs something like we expect:

```
$ node --harmony -e \
  'require("./lib/rdf-parser.js")("cache/epub/132/pg132.rdf", console.log)'
null { _id: 132,
  title: 'The Art of War',
  authors: [ 'Sunzi (6th cent. BC)', 'Giles, Lionel' ],
  subjects:
   [ 'Military art and science -- Early works to 1800',
     'War -- Early works to 1800' ] }
```

This is good for a first pass, but we can do better. Next let's see how to create a unit test for this module.

Unit Testing with Nodeunit

Let's create a unit test for our RDF parser module. This will confirm that it does what we believe it should, and will give us an opportunity to see how to do unit testing in Node.

There are many unit-testing frameworks available through npm. A few of the most popular ones are mocha,[5] vows,[6] and nodeunit.[7] We'll use nodeunit because it's a relatively simple unit-testing framework, with support for asynchronous tests and deep equality checks.

Many Node modules are meant to be used as a library, but some modules, like nodeunit, are intended to run as stand-alone programs on the command line, too. To install such a module globally, use npm's -g flag:

```
$ npm install -g nodeunit
```

---

4.   https://en.wikipedia.org/wiki/Library_of_Congress_Subject_Headings
5.   http://visionmedia.github.io/mocha/
6.   http://vowsjs.org/
7.   https://npmjs.org/package/nodeunit

You can confirm that it has been installed successfully by asking for its path through which:

```
$ which nodeunit
/usr/local/bin/nodeunit
```

Now let's make a unit test. Inside your database project directory, create a subdirectory called test. Then copy the pg132.rdf file into it.

```
$ mkdir test
$ cp cache/epub/132/pg132.rdf test/
```

Next, open a text editor and enter the following:

databases/test/pg132.json

```
{
  "_id": "132",
  "title": "The Art of War",
  "authors": [
    "Sunzi (6th cent. BC)",
    "Giles, Lionel"
  ],
  "subjects": [
    "Military art and science -- Early works to 1800",
    "War -- Early works to 1800"
  ]
}
```

Save this JSON file as test/pg132.json.

Now we can write a unit test that uses these fixtures. Open your editor and enter this:

databases/test/test-rdf-parser.js

```
'use strict';
const
  rdfParser = require('../lib/rdf-parser.js'),
  expectedValue = require('./pg132.json');
exports.testRDFParser = function(test) {
  rdfParser(__dirname + '/pg132.rdf', function(err, book) {
    test.expect(2);
    test.ifError(err);
    test.deepEqual(book, expectedValue, "book should match expected");
    test.done();
  });
};
```

Save this file as test-rdf-parser.js. This test module exposes one method called testRDFParser(), which uses the rdf-parser module to read and parse pg132.rdf. It then performs a deep equality check between the received object and the expected output as defined in pg132.json.

Note that here we're using require() to read the contents of a JSON file, as opposed to a Node module. For your convenience, when you require a file that ends in .json, Node will parse it and return the object as though it were assigned to exports.

Also, notice the _dirname variable used in finding the path to pg132.rdf. _dirname always points to the directory containing the module file being executed. Without this, the path would be calculated relative to the current working directory—where the nodeunit command was called from.

To execute the test, we run nodeunit through node --harmony and pass it the test/ directory:

```
$ node --harmony $(which nodeunit) test/
```

```
test-rdf-parser
✓ testRDFParser

OK: 2 assertions (437ms)
```

Great! Since our module only has one method, we'll leave the test as it is. If we had more methods to test, we could either add more exports to this test file, or add more files to the test directory.

Throttling Node.js

With our RDF parsing module in place and well tested, let's turn our attention to getting all those thousands of records into the database.

But one word of caution before we proceed: the code in this section attempts to demonstrate performance-related problems and their solutions. The speed of your hardware and the settings of your operating system may make it easier or harder to see these effects.

Alright—to crawl the cache directory, we'll use a module called file, which is available through npm.[8] Install and save it as usual, and we'll begin:

```
$ npm install --save file
```

The file module has a convenient method called walk() that traverses a directory tree and calls a callback for each file it finds.

Naive File Parsing at Scale

Let's use this method to find all the RDF files and send them through our RDF parser. Open a text editor and enter this:

---

8. https://npmjs.org/package/file

```
databases/list-books.js
'use strict';
const

  file = require('file'),
  rdfParser = require('./lib/rdf-parser.js');

console.log('beginning directory walk');

file.walk(__dirname + '/cache', function(err, dirPath, dirs, files){
  files.forEach(function(path){
    rdfParser(path, function(err, doc) {
      if (err) {
        throw err;
      } else {
        console.log(doc);
      }
    });
  });
});
```

Save the file as list-books.js in your databases project. This short program walks down the cache directory and passes each RDF file it finds into the RDF parser. The parser's callback just echoes the JSON out to the console if there wasn't an error.

Run the program, and let's see what it produces:

```
$ node --harmony list-books.js
beginning directory walk

./list-books.js:12
        throw err;
        ^
Error: EMFILE, open './cache/epub/12292/pg12292.rdf'
```

Failure! The problem here is masked by the innocuous-looking Error: EMFILE. This kind of error occurs when you've exhausted the number of file descriptors available on the system (typically just over 10,000).

There are a couple of ways to solve this problem. One way is to increase the maximum number of file descriptors in the operating system. However, that's only a temporary fix, until you run into even bigger file sets.

Another way would be to modify the rdf-parser module to retry when it receives an EMFILE error. A third-party module called graceful-fs does this, for example.[9]

---

9.   https://npmjs.org/package/graceful-fs

But you can't always count on your dependency modules to be graceful with file handling, so we'll use another approach: *work queuing*. Rather than immediately sending each file path into the RDF parser, we'll queue them as work to be done and let the queue throttle the number of concurrently running tasks.

Queuing to Limit Work in Progress

For this we'll use the async module.[10] Go ahead and install it now.

```
$ npm install --save async
```

Async offers low-overhead mechanisms for managing asynchronous code. For example, it has methods for executing a sequence of asynchronous tasks sequentially or in parallel, with a callback to invoke when they're all done.

We need the ability to run a whole bunch of tasks, but limit the number that are running at any time. For this we need async.queue().

Open your editor and enter this:

databases/list-books-queued.js
```
'use strict';
const

  async = require('async'),
  file = require('file'),
  rdfParser = require('./lib/rdf-parser.js'),

  work = async.queue(function(path, done) {
    rdfParser(path, function(err, doc) {
      console.log(doc);
      done();
    });
  }, 1000);

console.log('beginning directory walk');
file.walk(__dirname + '/cache', function(err, dirPath, dirs, files){
  files.forEach(function(path){
    work.push(path);
  });
});
```

Save this file as list-books-queued.js. Notice that we create a work object by passing async.queue() a worker function and a concurrency limit of 1,000. This object has a push() method that we use to add more paths for processing.

---

10. https://npmjs.org/package/async

The worker function we used to create the queue takes two arguments: path and done. The path argument is the path to an RDF file discovered by walking the directory tree. done is a callback that our worker function has to call to signal to the work queue that it's free to dequeue the next path.

In Node.js, it's common for the last argument to a callback to be a done or next function. Technically, you can name this argument whatever you want (it's your function, after all). But naming it done or next signals that this is a callback function that takes no arguments and should be called exactly once when you're finished doing whatever it is that you're doing. By contrast, callback functions named callback often take one or more arguments, starting with an err argument.

Now let's give this program a try and see if it works better. There may be a long pause between when you kick off the program and when you start seeing anything happen—this is to be expected.

```
$ node --harmony list-books-queued.js
{ _id: 0, title: '', authors: [], subjects: [] }
{ _id: 10,
  title: 'The Bible, Old and New Testaments, King James Version',
  authors: [],
  subjects: [ 'Religion' ] }
{ _id: 1,
  title: 'United States Declaration of Independence',
  authors: [ 'United States' ],
  subjects: [ 'United States -- History -- Revolution, 1775-1783 -- Sources' ] }
{ _id: 1000,
  title: 'La Divina Commedia di Dante',
  authors: [ 'Dante Alighieri' ],
  subjects: [ 'Poetry' ] }
...
```

Great! This program will run for quite a while if you let it. Instead, go ahead and kill it with Ctrl-C.

Now on to the last step: pumping these records into the database.

Putting It All Together

With a working parser and a throttled queue, we're ready to add the last piece: putting the records into the database.

Open your editor to the list-books-queued.js file one more time. First, add an extra require to the top of the file to pull in the request module like we did for the dbcli.js program. Then, find the callback we pass into rdfParser(). Replace what's there with this:

`databases/import-books.js`

```
rdfParser(path, function(err, doc) {
  request({
    method: 'PUT',
    url: 'http://localhost:5984/books/' + doc._id,
    json: doc
  }, function(err, res, body) {
    if (err) {
      throw Error(err);
    }
    console.log(res.statusCode, body);
    done();
  });
});
```

Save this new file as import-books.js. Instead of dumping the parsed object (doc) directly to the console, now we PUT it into the database using request(). Then we take the response we get from the database and send that to the console.

Time to find out if it works. Kick it off on the command line:

```
$ node --harmony import-books.js
beginning directory walk

./import-books.js:18
          throw Error(err);
              ^
Error: Error: write ECONNRESET
    at Error (<anonymous>)
    at Request._callback (./import-books.js:18:17)
    at self.callback (./node_modules/request/index.js:148:22)
    at Request.EventEmitter.emit (events.js:100:17)
...
```

Well, the error isn't EMFILE, so we didn't run out of file descriptors. The error ECONNRESET means that the TCP connection to the database died abruptly. This shouldn't be very surprising; we tried to open upwards of a thousand connections to it at the same time.

The easiest thing we can do is dial back the concurrency for the work queue. Rather than allowing 1,000 concurrent jobs, change it to only 10. When you're done, clear out the books database and try running the import again:

```
$ ./dbcli.js DELETE books
200 { ok: true }
$ ./dbcli.js PUT books
201 { ok: true }
$ node --harmony import-books.js
beginning directory walk
201 { ok: true, id: '0', rev: '1-453265faaa77a714d46bd72f62326186' }
```

```
201 { ok: true, id: '1', rev: '1-52a8081284aa74919298d724e5b73589' }
201 { ok: true,
  id: '10002',
  rev: '1-cf704abd67ec797f318dc6c949c7beed' }
201 { ok: true,
  id: '10000',
  rev: '1-4ccce019854dd45ba6a7c5c064c4460b' }
...
```

Recall that 201 is the HTTP status code for Created. The 201s above mean the database is successfully creating our documents.

This program will take quite a while to complete. You can check on its progress using the dbcli program we made earlier from a second terminal. Run ./dbcli.js GET books and look at the doc_count property in the output to see how many records have been imported.

Dealing with Update Conflicts

But one more thing before we move on to querying. There's something strange about that first entry—let's take a look at book 0:

```
$ ./dbcli.js GET books/0
200 { _id: '0',
  _rev: '1-453265faaa77a714d46bd72f62326186',
  title: '',
  authors: [],
  subjects: [] }
```

The book with id 0 has no title, no authors, and no subjects. It turns out that this record is just a template; the RDF file that produced this document is pretty much empty.

We don't need this document, so let's delete it. Try removing it with DELETE:

```
$ ./dbcli.js DELETE books/0
409 { error: 'conflict', reason: 'Document update conflict.' }
```

CouchDB responded with a 409 Conflict status code. This is actually a good thing—CouchDB guards against conflicts and race conditions by demanding a revision ID for updates to an existing document. Since our request didn't include a rev parameter at all, it didn't match the document we were attempting to delete.

So, to DELETE or PUT a document that exists, you need to provide a revision:

```
$ ./dbcli.js DELETE books/0?rev=1-453265faaa77a714d46bd72f62326186
200 { ok: true, id: '0', rev: '2-1ab4213771c4fbf4c48e11c246e8a6fc' }
```

Different databases and RESTful services deal with conflicts differently. Relying on a rev parameter is a characteristic specific to CouchDB.

With that extra document out of the way, it's time to start querying the data.

Querying Data with Mapreduce Views

Different databases offer different ways of querying data, but most include some concept of *indexing*. When you index data in a database, you make it available for quick retrieval by some field or attribute of the data.

With CouchDB, you write mapreduce functions, which produce *views*. A view is a kind of index that maps values back to documents. With a view, you can query for documents with particular attributes or fields—like finding a book by its author.

We'll create two views for our Gutenberg data set: one for finding books by author, and one for finding books on a given subject. Since CouchDB views consist of JavaScript code, we'll keep them in a Node.js module and write a small utility program for loading them into CouchDB.

Cross-Environment Scripting with Node

Most of the time when you write JavaScript code, you intend for that code to be executed in the same *environment* in which you wrote it. For example, if you write a method in a Node module, you probably expect that some future Node process will run that function.

Sometimes, though, the JavaScript code you write might be destined for a different environment. I call this *cross-environment scripting*—writing JavaScript in one environment but executing it in another. In our case, we'll be writing functions in Node that we intend to run in CouchDB.

Let's write the view code. Open a text editor and enter this:

```
databases/lib/views.js
module.exports = {
  by_author: {
    map: function(doc) {
      if ('authors' in doc) {
        doc.authors.forEach(emit);
      }
    }.toString(),
    reduce: '_count'
  },

  by_subject: {
    map: function(doc) {
```

```
    if ('subjects' in doc) {
      doc.subjects.forEach(function(subject){
        emit(subject, subject);

        subject.split(/\s+--\s+/).forEach(function(part){
          emit(part, subject);
        });
      });
    }
  }.toString(),

  reduce: '_count'
  }
};
```

Save this file in your project's lib directory as views.js.

The first view is the by_author view—this will let us find books by a particular author. Its map() function emits a key for each author of each document that has an authors array (that is, each book we've imported). We have to check whether the document has an authors key in case the database has any documents that aren't books.

The second view is by_subject. For each subject in the subjects array, we emit the whole subject as well as each part (separated by two dashes). For example, say a book has the subject *"Assassins – Drama"*. The by_subject mapper would emit *"Assassins – Drama"*, *"Assassins"*, and *"Drama"*. This lets us find books by full or partial subject.

Both views' map functions have to be encoded as strings so we can put them into CouchDB, since it allows only JSON documents (and true functions are not allowed in JSON). The reduce function for both views is CouchDB's built-in _count function. This will let us find out how many books are available by a particular author, or in a particular subject.

Now let's get these views into the database.

Callback Chaining with async.waterfall

CouchDB stores views in special documents called *design documents*. You use regular REST commands to add and remove design documents, just like you would any other document. So we need to PUT into CouchDB a design document that contains our views.

Let's write a script that creates or updates a design document to house these views. Open your editor again and enter this:

databases/make-views.js

```
#!/usr/bin/env node --harmony
'use strict';
const
  async = require('async'),
  request = require('request'),
  views = require('./lib/views.js');
async.waterfall([

  // get the existing design doc (if present)
  function(next) {
    request.get('http://localhost:5984/books/_design/books', next);
  },

  // create a new design doc or use existing
  function(res, body, next) {
    if (res.statusCode === 200) {
      next(null, JSON.parse(body));
    } else if (res.statusCode === 404) {
      next(null, { views: {} });
    }
  },

  // add views to document and submit
  function(doc, next) {
    Object.keys(views).forEach(function(name) {
      doc.views[name] = views[name];
    });
    request({
      method: 'PUT',
      url: 'http://localhost:5984/books/_design/books',
      json: doc
    }, next);
  }
], function(err, res, body) {
  if (err) { throw err; }
  console.log(res.statusCode, body);
});
```

Save the file as make-views.js in your project directory and make the file executable using chmod in a terminal. This program uses the async module's waterfall() method to execute a sequence of asynchronous functions. Using the waterfall method cleans up code that would otherwise have to be highly indented due to nested callbacks.

waterfall() takes two arguments: an array of functions to execute sequentially and a summary function to call when everything is finished. Each function in the array takes some number of arguments and finally a next callback to pass results forward into the next function.

Our first function kicks off a request for the design document called _design/books, using the next function as its callback. If this is your first time running this program, there won't be a _desing/books document yet and the request will return a 404 Not Found status code.

The second function checks to see whether we got a 404 Not Found or a 200 OK. For a 200 OK, we just want to parse out the JSON returned in the response body and pass that forward. For a 404 Not Found, we have to create a skeleton design document to pass to the next function.

The third function copies the views we put in the views.js module onto the design document. Then it issues a PUT request to the database to save the newly created or updated document. Like our earlier request, we use the next function for the callback to request().

Finally, the summary function reports the returned status code and response body from the last request. This will produce output just like our dbcli.js program.

Let's try it out! Open a terminal and run make-views.js:

```
$ ./make-views.js
201 { ok: true,
  id: '_design/books',
  rev: '1-7e273ea81e766d078ea17f0c4950fe2a' }
```

OK, cool—the design doc is in the database. Now we should be able to query the views. Like all gestures in CouchDB, querying a view is done via REST.

For example, we can get a list of all authors and the number of books to their name. We do this by getting the _design/books document with the special suffix _view/by_author to tell CouchDB that we want the results of the generated view:

```
$ ./dbcli.js GET books/_design/books/_view/by_author?group=true
200 { rows:
  [ { key: '"Colored Quartet" (name unknown)', value: 1 },
    { key: '(Mrs.) L. P.', value: 1 },
    { key: '`Abdu\'l-Bahá', value: 19 },
    { key: 'A Gentleman of Elvas [pseud.]', value: 1 },
    { key: 'A--a', value: 1 },
    { key: 'A-No. 1', value: 1 },
    { key: 'A. C. F.', value: 1 },
    { key: 'A. L. O. E.', value: 5 },
    { key: 'A.E.', value: 2 },
...
```

It may take a while for the results to come back, especially if you just recently added the _design/books document. To process the map function,

CouchDB sends every document in the database through it to produce the view. As new documents are added, CouchDB will incrementally update the generated views (it doesn't have to run through them all each time).

The group=true parameter tells CouchDB that we want the result of running the reduce function as well. Since our reduce function is a basic count, the value field of each row is the number of books attributed to that author. So, for example, the author *"A.E."* is credited with two books.

CouchDB allows you to ask for a subset of view records by specifying a specific key or a startkey and endkey as URL parameters. We'll use these capabilities in Chapter 6, *Scalable Web Services*, on page 87, when we build our own RESTful interface for querying the data.

Wrapping Up

This chapter covered a lot of ground against the backdrop of working with databases. To start, we created a project directory complete with a package.json file for managing dependencies through npm.

By choosing CouchDB—a RESTful, JSON-based, document-oriented data-store—we got a detailed look at how RESTful APIs work. We used the request module to simplify making HTTP client requests from Node.

Step by step, you created scripts to import large amounts of data into CouchDB with Node. We saw how Node's extreme speed sometimes works against it, exhausting system resources and overwhelming other services. To fix this, we explored techniques for queuing work using the async module. Along the way you learned how to use nodeunit to develop and run unit tests for your modules.

Robustness

We dealt with the ECONNRESET problem in *Putting It All Together*, on page 78, by turning the concurrency down from 1,000 to 10.

- What would happen if we still got an ECONNRESET?
- How would you change the code to retry the operation?

CHAPTER 6

Scalable Web Services

A lot of the buzz around Node.js centers on using it for writing scalable web-sites, apps, and services. In this chapter we'll develop robust, RESTful, JavaScript Object Notation (JSON)-based web services. Creating web services will be our backdrop for digging into these aspects of Node development:

Architecture and Core
> You'll learn how to use Node's built-in http module to create a basic HTTP server.

Patterns
> Some Node modules have their own ecosystem of plug-ins that provide additional behavior. We'll use plug-ins for Express and learn how its middleware pattern provides hooks for additional functionality. We'll also use promises, a powerful abstraction for writing asynchronous code.

JavaScriptisms
> ECMAScript Harmony introduces new concepts called iterators and generators. You'll learn how to create and use generators, and how they combine with promises to simplify asynchronous programming.

Supporting Code
> For our project, we'll use more features of npm, like specifying scripts to start our project. We'll also use nodemon to monitor our Node programs and automatically restart them when the source changes.

Node.js comes with support for low-overhead HTTP servers out of the box using the http module.[1] But writing services against the low-level http module directly can be a lot of work. So we'll use Express for developing our web services.[2]

---

1. http://nodejs.org/api/http.html
2. http://expressjs.com/

Because the code samples are getting more involved, you should go grab the code download that comes with this book rather than trying to type it all in. In the code download, you'll find a web-services directory that contains all the code from this chapter. Go get it now if you don't have it, then let's get started with Express.

Advantages of Express

Express is a web application framework for Node modeled after the Ruby project Sinatra.[3] Express provides a lot of the plumbing code that you'd otherwise end up writing yourself. To see why, let's take a look at a basic Node.js server using only the http module.

web-services/server.js
```
const
  http = require('http'),
  server = http.createServer(function(req, res) {
    res.writeHead(200, {'Content-Type': 'text/plain'});
    res.end('Hello World\n');
  });
server.listen(3000, function(){
  console.log('ready captain!');
});
```

This is quite similar to creating a basic TCP server using the net module. First we bring in the http module, call its createServer() method with a callback, and finally use server.listen() to bind a TCP socket for listening. The callback function uses information from the incoming HTTP request (req) to send an appropriate response (res).

What's remarkable about this example isn't what it does, but rather what it doesn't do. There are lots of little jobs a typical web server would take care of that this code doesn't touch. Here are some examples:

* Routing based on URL paths
* Managing sessions via cookies
* Parsing incoming requests (like form data or JSON)
* Rejecting malformed requests

The Express framework helps with these and myriad other tasks.

Serving APIs with Express

As for all Node modules, to use Express you have to install it with npm. The example project we're working from already specifies a dependency on Express,

---

3.   http://www.sinatrarb.com/

so all we have to do is run npm install. If you were making your own project, you'd want to run npm install --save express to pull down the latest Express available and record the dependency in your package.json file.

Let's take a look at a Hello World Express app to get a feel for how it works. Then we'll expand on this skeleton to make our own RESTful APIs. In the terminal, navigate to the hello subdirectory of the example project. Here is the content of the server.js file you'll find there:

```
web-services/hello/server.js
#!/usr/bin/env node --harmony
'use strict';
const
  express = require('express'),
  app = express();
app.use(express.logger('dev'));
app.get('/api/:name', function(req, res) {
  res.json(200, { "hello": req.params.name });
});
app.listen(3000, function(){
  console.log("ready captain.");
});
```

First, this program brings in the express module and creates an app. Like the request module we worked with in the last chapter, the express module is itself a function. When you call this function, Express creates an application context for you. By convention, we name this variable app.

Express functionality is provided through something called *middleware*, which are asynchronous functions that manipulate the request and response objects. To specify middleware for your app, you call app.use(), passing in the middleware you want. In our case, we're using the logger middleware set to dev mode, which will log to the console all requests coming in.

Next we use app.get() to tell Express how we want to handle HTTP GET requests to the /api/:name path. The :name chunk in the path is called a *named route parameter*. When the API is hit, Express will grab that part of the URL and make it available in req.params.

In addition to get(), Express has put(), post(), and del() to register handlers for PUT, POST, and DELETE requests, respectively. In our case, we tell the response object, res, to send back as JSON an object whose hello key is set to the name parameter.

Finally, this program listens on TCP port 3000 for incoming HTTP requests, and logs a message to the console when it's ready to receive connections. Let's run the app to see what it does.

Running a Server with npm

Instead of starting the server with node directly, this time we'll use npm. Open a terminal to the hello directory and run npm start:

```
$ npm start

> hello@0.1.0 start ./hello
> node --harmony server.js

ready captain.
```

npm knows how to run this server because of the scripts hash in the package.json file. If you open the package.json, you'll find a section that looks like this:

```
"scripts": {
  "start": "node --harmony ./server.js"
},
```

You can add more scripts to the scripts hash—for example, it's common to add a test item so that you can run npm test to execute your project's unit tests.

Testing REST Endpoints with curl

With the Hello server running, let's try it out. In a separate console, request the /api/* path with curl:

```
$ curl -i http://localhost:3000/api/jimbo
HTTP/1.1 200 OK
X-Powered-By: Express
Content-Type: application/json
Content-Length: 22
Date: Tue, 10 Sep 2013 14:41:22 GMT
Connection: keep-alive

{
  "hello": "jimbo"
}
```

curl is a useful command-line tool for issuing HTTP requests to a given server. Adding the -i flag tells curl that it should output the HTTP headers in addition to the JSON body. Back in the server terminal, you should see this (thanks to the logger middleware):

```
GET /api/ 200 7ms - 22b
```

OK, now that we've got the basic outline of an Express REST service under control, let's build something with a bit more bite to it.

Writing Modular Express Services

Throughout the remainder of the chapter, we're going to build a RESTful web service with Express for creating and managing *book bundles*. These are basically named reading lists. Our app will be called Better Book Bundle Builder (or b4 for short).

We'll work extensively with the books database we set up in Chapter 5, *Accessing Databases*, on page 65, as well as a new database called b4. Our application will work roughly as follows:

- It will communicate with two databases: the books database and the b4 database.

- To the b4 application, the books database is read-only (we will not add, delete, or overwrite any documents in it).

- The b4 database will store user data, including the book bundles that users make.

To create the b4 database, make sure CouchDB is running, then use curl from the command line:

```
$ curl -X PUT http://localhost:5984/b4
{"ok":true}
```

The -X flag lets you specify which HTTP method to use. We'll use curl a lot in this chapter for testing our web services.

Now we're ready to create our modular, RESTful web services.

Separating Server Code into Modules

Just like our Hello World example, the main entry point for the b4 service is the server.js file. But instead of assigning a handler with app.get() directly, now we specify some configuration parameters and pull in the API modules.

Here's the part of b4/server.js that differs from the Hello World version:

```
web-services/b4/server.js
const config = {
  bookdb: 'http://localhost:5984/books/',
  b4db: 'http://localhost:5984/b4/'
};

require('./lib/book-search.js')(config, app);
require('./lib/field-search.js')(config, app);
require('./lib/bundle.js')(config, app);
```

Each of the three API modules is a function that takes two arguments: our config hash and the Express app to add routes to.

Let's run the server and then we'll dig into the API modules. This time, instead of using npm start, we'll use nodemon. Short for "Node Monitor," nodemon runs a Node.js program and then automatically restarts it whenever the source code changes.

To get nodemon, install it globally through npm:

```
$ npm install -g nodemon
```

Now use nodemon to start up the b4 service.

```
$ nodemon --harmony server.js
16 Sep 19:05:50 - [nodemon] v0.7.8
16 Sep 19:05:50 - [nodemon] to restart at any time, enter `rs`
16 Sep 19:05:50 - [nodemon] watching: ./web-services/b4
16 Sep 19:05:50 - [nodemon] starting `node --harmony server.js`
ready captain.
```

Now let's dig into the search APIs.

Implementing Search APIs

To build a book bundle, a user has to be able to discover books to add to it. So our modular web service will have two search APIs: field search (for discovering authors and subjects) and book search (for finding books by a given author or subject).

The Node.js code for these two APIs is quite similar—so we'll focus on the field search here and leave the book search for the wrap-up questions at the end.

The field search API helps users to find authors or subjects based on a starting string. For example, to get a list of subjects that start with Croc, you'd make a request like this:

```
$ curl http://localhost:3000/api/search/subject?q=Croc
[
  "Crocheting",
  "Crocheting -- Patterns",
  "Crockett, Davy, 1786-1836",
  "Crocodiles",
  "Crocodiles -- Juvenile fiction"
]
```

This API could be employed, for instance, in a user interface so that when a user starts typing a subject, suggestions automatically pop up.

```
web-services/b4/lib/field-search.js
Line 1  'use strict';
     -  const request = require('request');
     -  module.exports = function(config, app) {
     -    app.get('/api/search/:view', function(req, res) {
     5      request({
     -        method: 'GET',
     -        url: config.bookdb + '_design/books/_view/by_' + req.params.view,
     -        qs: {
     -          startkey: JSON.stringify(req.query.q),
    10          endkey: JSON.stringify(req.query.q + "\ufff0"),
     -          group: true
     -        }
     -      }, function(err, couchRes, body) {
     -
    15        // couldn't connect to CouchDB
     -        if (err) {
     -          res.json(502, { error: "bad_gateway", reason: err.code });
     -          return;
     -        }
    20
     -        // CouchDB couldn't process our request
     -        if (couchRes.statusCode !== 200) {
     -          res.json(couchRes.statusCode, JSON.parse(body));
     -          return;
    25        }
     -
     -        // send back just the keys we got back from CouchDB
     -        res.json(JSON.parse(body).rows.map(function(elem){
     -          return elem.key;
    30        }));
     -
     -      });
     -    });
     -  };
```

This program does a lot in a small space. Let's dig into it a piece at a time.

First, in line 3, we set module.exports to a function. This is how we create a module that is itself a function (like request and express). When you write modules that do just one thing, this is a handy pattern.

Next up, we call app.get() in line 4 to register a route with the Express app. Once the route callback function starts, it immediately makes a request to CouchDB, starting on line 5. To build out the request URL, we use the value in req.params.view, which Express extracted from the URL.

So, for instance, when someone requests /api/search/subject, this will trigger a request to the CouchDB view _design/books/_view/by_subject. Notice that we don't check whether req.params.view is one of our expected values—this is left as an exercise at the end of the chapter.

To limit the results coming back from CouchDB, we specify query string parameters in the qs object. We pull the incoming URL parameter q on line 9. When an incoming request contains ?q=Croc, then req.query.q will be the string "Croc" (without quotes).

When receiving a request for a view, CouchDB uses the startkey and endkey parameters to bind the results. In our case, we want all the keys that start with the query string. Using req.query.q + "\ufff0" for the endkey guarantees that we'll get all the keys that start with our query param. And setting group to true for this view tells CouchDB that we want unique keys only (no duplicates).

Finally, starting on line 13, we have our handler function for when the CouchDB request returns. There are three outcomes we have to account for:

- The error case—CouchDB didn't respond, so we should send 502 Bad Gateway back to the requester.

- The non-success case—CouchDB responded, but it wasn't the HTTP 200 OK result that we expected, so we pass it verbatim back to the requester.

- The success case—CouchDB responded with the data we're after, so we parse the JSON and extract just the keys to send back.

This example demonstrates some of the challenges you'll face writing RESTful APIs. The nice thing about REST is that it gives you a good basis for an API. For a variety of cases, the HTTP specification prescribes very specific status codes.[4]

However, doing it right can be a challenge since you have to account for a variety of success and non-success cases. Promises offer one way of managing asynchronous code that can help with these challenges, as we'll see in upcoming sections as we build out more RESTful APIs.

RESTful APIs with Promises

One thing I really love about JavaScript is its extreme flexibility. In JavaScript there are seven different ways of doing anything, and you get to pick the one you like. This is especially true of managing asynchronous code.

---

4. http://www.w3.org/Protocols/rfc2616/rfc2616-sec10.html

We've already seen a number of approaches to working with asynchronous code in JavaScript. Early on, we used regular Node.js callbacks, and then talked about EventEmitters and streams. We explored the async module and its suite of asynchronous coding utilities, as well.

Now let's turn to the RESTful APIs for editing book bundles. Here we'll talk about promises—another approach to managing asynchronous code.

Creating a Resource through POST with a Promise

The first thing we'll need for our bundle API is a way to create them. For that, we'll create an Express route that handles POST requests. Inside the handler, we'll use a promise to keep track of the request.

Whenever a regular JavaScript function starts executing, it will finish in one of two ways: either it will run to completion, or it will throw an exception. For synchronous code, this is good enough; but for asynchronous code we need a bit more. Node.js callbacks use two arguments to reflect these two cases (e.g., function(err, data){...}), and EventEmitters use different event types.

A *promise* is an object that encapsulates these two results for an asynchronous operation. Once the operation is completed, the promise will either be resolved (success case) or rejected (error case). You use the then() method to attach success and error handlers to a promise.

Let's see how this works by using a promise with the result of a request() to our CouchDB server. There are many promise libraries available through npm—we'll use kriskowal's Q module.[5] Q is a full-featured promise library with lots of helper methods for interoperating with different asynchronous code-management approaches.

Open the lib/bundle.js file and take a look. At the top, you'll see that we bring in the request and Q modules.

Then, inside the module.exports function, you'll find the following code. It's the source of the POST handler for creating a bundle:

web-services/b4/lib/bundle.js
```
Line 1  app.post('/api/bundle', function(req, res) {
   -      let deferred = Q.defer();
   -      request.post({
   -        url: config.b4db,
   5        json: { type: 'bundle', name: req.query.name, books: {} }
   -      }, function(err, couchRes, body) {
```

---

5.   https://npmjs.org/package/q

```
        if (err) {
          deferred.reject(err);
10      } else {
          deferred.resolve([couchRes, body]);
        }
      });

15    deferred.promise.then(function(args) {
        let couchRes = args[0], body = args[1];
        res.json(couchRes.statusCode, body);
      }, function(err) {
        res.json(502, { error: "bad_gateway", reason: err.code });
20    });
    });
```

This code adds a route using app.post() that sends forward a POST to CouchDB and returns its results. You can try it out with curl like so:

```
$ curl -X POST http://localhost:3000/api/bundle/
{
  "ok": true,
  "id": "9122b028cd8683df0813b0fc69000377",
  "rev": "1-7ef008d5d399c6ba0b1602e09434406f"
}
```

In line 2, we create a Deferred object. This class is something specific to the Q module—it provides methods for working with the promise.

When the request eventually finishes, we'll either reject the promise, passing forward the error (line 9), or we'll resolve the promise, passing along the CouchDB response and body (line 11).

Meanwhile, in line 15, we call the promise's then() method, passing in two functions. The first function will be called when the promise is resolved (success). The second function will be called if the promise happens to be rejected.

Although there's nothing to stop you from creating Deferred objects in this way, you usually don't have to. Instead, Q offers shortcut methods that produce promises for you when you're working with familiar patterns like Node callbacks. Let's see how these work next, as we write an API for retrieving a bundle.

Retrieving a Resource through GET and nfcall()

Still working from lib/bundle.js, let's see the router for GET requests for a bundle. Like the POST handler we just looked at, this implementation uses a promise for the request to CouchDB, but it doesn't explicitly create a Deferred object.

```
web-services/b4/lib/bundle.js
Line 1  app.get('/api/bundle/:id', function(req, res) {
     2    Q.nfcall(request.get, config.b4db + '/' + req.params.id)
     3      .then(function(args) {
     4        let couchRes = args[0], bundle = JSON.parse(args[1]);
     5        res.json(couchRes.statusCode, bundle);
     6      }, function(err) {
     7        res.json(502, { error: "bad_gateway", reason: err.code });
     8      })
     9      .done();
    10  });
```

You can call this API with curl by passing in the ID of a previously created bundle.

```
$ curl http://localhost:3000/api/bundle/9122b028cd8683df0813b0fc69000377
{
  "_id": "9122b028cd8683df0813b0fc69000377",
  "_rev": "1-7ef008d5d399c6ba0b1602e09434406f",
  "type": "bundle",
  "books": {}
}
```

In line 1, we create an Express route for /api/bundle/:id with app.get(). But then in line 2, instead of calling request() directly, we call Q.nfcall(request.get...).

Q's nfcall() method is short for "Node Function Call." It takes a function that expects a regular Node.js callback as its last parameter (like request()), invokes the function, and returns a promise. In effect, it does automatically what our POST handler did explicitly by creating a Deferred.

After that, we call the promise's then() method with success and failure handlers just as before. And lastly we call done() on the promise chain to force any unhandled rejected promises to throw.

In Node.js, promises have a habit of swallowing errors. Calling done() on a promise chain is Q's Golden Rule—whenever you make a promise, you should either return it so someone else can deal with it, or call done.

When you have only one promise, it's not clear how the abstraction helps with managing asynchronous code. The benefits start to become more obvious when you have a chain of asynchronous operations that you need to manage.

Updating a Resource through PUT with Chained Promises

We've looked at a couple of GET routes and one POST so far. Here we'll examine the code to update a bundle's name property, which uses HTTP PUT.

This code uses promises to manage asynchronous behavior to an even greater extent than previous APIs we've seen. Here's the code for the PUT route that powers setting a bundle's name:

```
web-services/b4/lib/bundle.js
```

```
Line 1   app.put('/api/bundle/:id/name/:name', function(req, res) {
    -       Q.nfcall(request.get, config.b4db + '/' + req.params.id)
    -         .then(function(args) {
    -           let couchRes = args[0], bundle = JSON.parse(args[1]);
  5             if (couchRes.statusCode !== 200) {
    -             return [couchRes, bundle];
    -           }

    -           bundle.name = req.params.name;
 10             return Q.nfcall(request.put, {
    -             url: config.b4db + '/' + req.params.id,
    -             json: bundle
    -           });
    -         })
 15         .then(function(args) {
    -           let couchRes = args[0], body = args[1];
    -           res.json(couchRes.statusCode, body);
    -         })
    -         .catch(function(err) {
 20           res.json(502, { error: "bad_gateway", reason: err.code });
    -         })
    -         .done();
    -   });
```

This endpoint starts off much like the GET bundle API. It invokes request.get through Q.nfcall() to make a promise, and proceeds to use the then() method to handle the response. So far so good.

Now, an important thing to understand about then() is that it returns a new promise that will be fulfilled or rejected depending on what happens in then's success and failure callbacks. In other words, when you call then() on a promise, you set up a *promise chain*; each promise depends on the one that came before.

This REST handler has two calls to then()—one on line 3 and the other on line 15. The second then's handlers will be called depending on how the first one goes.

So let's take a look at the first then's callback. Once we extract the couchRes and bundle from the args array, we check to see if we got the 200 OK status code we were hoping for. If not, on line 6 we return an array with the couchRes and bundle. Q interprets this return statement as a successful resolution of the promise and calls the second then's handler function.

If we get the 200 OK status we're after, then the function continues to over-write the bundle's name field. We do another Q.nfcall() to PUT the bundle document back into CouchDB, and return the promise that this produces on line 10. Q waits for this subpromise to finish, then uses its value to resolve the original promise, at which point the second then's handler gets invoked.

So in either case—whether we return a value directly or another promise—Q knows what to do.

Lastly, notice the catch() method at the end of the promise chain on line 19. catch() is like then() except that it only takes an error handler, not a success handler. The catch handler will be called if any of the promises up the chain are rejected (either explicitly or by a function throwing an exception).

The name catch is not a coincidence. Just like a try/catch block lets you cap-ture exceptions in synchronous code, the catch handler lets you capture exceptions in promise-driven asynchronous code.

Promises are a powerful abstraction for working with asynchronous code, but to use them effectively you really need a firm grasp of how they work. They offer the possibility of simplifying your asynchronous workflow, especially when combined with another powerful abstraction: generators.

Next let's explore how generators work and see how they work with promises to make code that reads like it's synchronous but runs asynchronously.

Yielding Control with Generators

ECMAScript Harmony introduces a new concept called a *generator*. A gener-ator is like a function except that you can suspend its execution and resume later.

This feature isn't quite ready for prime time, and you'll need a version of Node higher than 0.10.x to try it out (unstable 0.11, for example). However, this is the direction ECMAScript is heading, and it'll be production-ready before you know it.

Once a regular JavaScript function starts executing, it can finish in one of two ways. Either it finishes normally by getting to the end or hitting a return statement, or it finishes abnormally, throwing an exception. In both cases, the function will run to conclusion.

Generators are different. With a generator, you can *yield* a value without actually finishing execution, and then pick up where you left off.

Counting Down with a Generator

Let's see how this works with a short example. Open your text editor and
enter this:

```
web-services/countdown.js
'use strict';
const
  countdown = function* (count) {
    while (count > 0) {
      yield count;
      count -= 1;
    }
  },

  counter = countdown(5),

  callback = function(){
    let item = counter.next();
    if (!item.done) {
      console.log(item.value);
      setTimeout(callback, 1000);
    }
  };
callback();
```

Save the file as countdown.js. This program counts down from five at one-second
intervals, sending each value to the console:

```
$ node --harmony countdown.js
5
4
3
2
1
```

The countdown() function is a *generator function*. The asterisk (*) in function*() is
what tells the JavaScript engine to treat this function differently.

When you call countdown with a starting value, what you get back is a generator.
In our case, we call countdown with 5 and store the generator to a variable called
counter.

The code inside the generator function starts executing the first time you call
the generator's next() method. It runs until it hits a yield, then sends back that
value.

Our example calls counter.next() inside of a function called callback. This callback
function saves the object returned by counter.next() into a variable called item.
This object has two properties of note:

- done—either true or false; indicates whether the generator function has run to completion.

- value—the last value yielded or returned.

So the callback function checks whether the generator still has more to do, and if so, logs the yielded value and sets a timeout to check again in one second.

Generators and Asynchronous Code

Because generators can pause their execution indefinitely, they offer a clever way to deal with asynchronous code. The countdown example doesn't show it, but inside your generator function, you can grab the value coming in through yield.

For example, say your generator function contains the following line:

```
let x = yield;
```

In this case, the value of x would be whatever was passed into generator.next() while it was suspended on the yield. So if you called generator.next(8), then x would be 8.

When the generator function and the calling code cooperate, you can do some really neat things. Consider this line from a hypothetical generator function:

```
let data = yield "./my-text-file.txt";
```

This line suspends execution after yielding the string "./my-text-file.txt" and expects to continue when it receives the data from that file. If the calling code knows to treat the string as a filename, it could do something like fs.readFile() and then pass the data back to the generator with generator.next(data).

It turns out that promises are a great fit for achieving this kind of coordination, as we'll see next.

Using Generators with Promises

Let's return to our Express APIs for working with book bundles. So far we have ways of creating and retrieving bundles, and we can update the name property of a bundle.

Now we'll make an API for adding books to a bundle using the PUT HTTP verb. This code will have to make several asynchronous calls: one to get the existing bundle, one to get book details, and one to put the bundle data back. To do all this, we'll use promises and generators to flatten and simplify the chain of operations.

Using the PUT book API

Before we get into the code, let's take a look at how this API works. That way, when we dive into the code it'll be more clear what it's doing.

To use the PUT book API, we need a bundle, so make one with the POST API through curl:

```
$ curl -X POST http://localhost:3000/api/bundle?name=War%20Books
{
  "ok": true,
  "id": "d476de5d13555f2e8dd0eaac7c000984",
  "rev": "1-d90a9d2a08880d9f29e6fa4515702d50"
}
```

Request the bundle with GET to see what's in it so far (your bundle ID may be different):

```
$ curl http://localhost:3000/api/bundle/d476de5d13555f2e8dd0eaac7c000984
{
  "_id": "d476de5d13555f2e8dd0eaac7c000984",
  "_rev": "1-d90a9d2a08880d9f29e6fa4515702d50",
  "type": "bundle",
  "name": "War Books",
  "books": {}
}
```

Then, let's add Sunzi's *The Art of War* (Project Gutenberg ID 132):

```
$ curl -X PUT \
  http://localhost:3000/api/bundle/d476de5d13555f2e8dd0eaac7c000984/book/132
{
  "ok": true,
  "id": "d476de5d13555f2e8dd0eaac7c000984",
  "rev": "2-537b36e10212810fa3d081a9afc64282"
}
```

Finally, let's see what was added to the bundle:

```
$ curl http://localhost:3000/api/bundle/d476de5d13555f2e8dd0eaac7c000984
{
  "_id": "d476de5d13555f2e8dd0eaac7c000984",
  "_rev": "2-537b36e10212810fa3d081a9afc64282",
  "type": "bundle",
  "name": "War Books",
  "books": {
    "132": "The Art of War"
  }
}
```

Success! The "War Books" bundle now contains *The Art of War*.

Let's take a look at the PUT handler that made this happen. This will be the last code block we inspect in the chapter, but it's also the most complex.

Yielding Promises with Q.async

Here's the section of lib/bundle.js that implements adding a book to a bundle with PUT:

web-services/b4/lib/bundle.js

```
app.put('/api/bundle/:id/book/:pgid', function(req, res) {

  let
    get = Q.denodeify(request.get),
    put = Q.denodeify(request.put);

  Q.async(function* (){
    let args, couchRes, bundle, book;

    // grab the bundle from the b4 database
    args = yield get(config.b4db + req.params.id);
    couchRes = args[0];
    bundle = JSON.parse(args[1]);

    // fail fast if we couldn't retrieve the bundle
    if (couchRes.statusCode !== 200) {
      res.json(couchRes.statusCode, bundle);
      return;
    }

    // look up the book by its Project Gutenberg ID
    args = yield get(config.bookdb + req.params.pgid);
    couchRes = args[0];
    book = JSON.parse(args[1]);

    // fail fast if we couldn't retrieve the book
    if (couchRes.statusCode !== 200) {
      res.json(couchRes.statusCode, book);
      return;
    }

    // add the book to the bundle and put it back in CouchDB
    bundle.books[book._id] = book.title;
    args = yield put({url: config.b4db + bundle._id, json: bundle});
    res.json(args[0].statusCode, args[1]);

  })()
  .catch(function(err) {
    res.json(502, { error: "bad_gateway", reason: err.code });
  });
});
```

The first thing to notice is line 4, where we call Q.denodeify() for request.get and request.put. The denodeify() method takes a Node.js-style function (one that expects a callback) and returns a new promise-producing function from it. Using denodeify is a convenient way to avoid calling Q.nfcall() all over the place. Instead, you just denodeify the functions you plan to use, and call them later knowing they'll produce promises.

Right after that, in line 7, we call Q.async() with a generator function. Q's async method returns a new promise-producing function that will start running the generator when you invoke it. We invoke this function right away on line 37.

Inside the generator, any time we yield a promise, Q will wait for the promise to resolve, then resume execution with the resolved value. For example, on line 11, we yield a promise for a get call to CouchDB. When the request finishes, the promise is resolved and Q gives us back the value, which we assign to args. This is much like the calls to then(function(args){...}) we saw earlier, but written in a more linear style.

If the HTTP status code from CouchDB was something other than the 200 OK we were hoping for, we send it back to the requester verbatim and return early. Otherwise, we move on to the second asynchronous call in line 22. Again we yield a promise for a get call to CouchDB, and again we check that everything was OK when it comes back.

Finally, on line 33, we add the book to the bundle and yield again—this time waiting on a put. When the put is finished, we send the results back to the requester. And if anything went wrong during all of this asynchronousness, we catch it on line 38.

This API makes three asynchronous requests, but does it in only one function thanks to Q.async and generator functions. On the plus side, writing code in this way has the potential to make it look like synchronous, linear code. But reaping this benefit means working deeply with promises and relying on some seemingly magical coordination logic.

Wrapping Up

This chapter took us on a crash course through writing RESTful APIs with Express. You learned how to create an Express-based web service and how to modularize your endpoints into separate files. You saw how to add script commands to npm and how to use nodemon for restarting your service as you make changes.

We also dug deep into promises, a novel way for managing asynchronous code. We used the Q library to create and chain promises, and handle error cases where promises are revoked. You also saw how to convert Node.js-style functions—which expect a callback—into promise-generating functions.

Finally, we used ECMAScript Harmony's generator functions with Q to write synchronous-looking code that's actually asynchronous. Although this code is easy to read, it masks some powerful logic that goes on behind the scenes.

We saw how Express's route methods (get(), post(), and friends) provide an easy way to set up path-based routing. And we used Express middleware to easily provide logging capabilities to all our routes.

You can do a whole lot more with Express and middleware than we covered in this chapter. In Chapter 7, *Web Apps*, on page 107, we'll build on what we have here as we create a web-based client for using our book and bundle APIs.

Code Organization

Take a look at the lib/book-search.js file included in the code for this chapter. It's nearly identical to lib/field-search.js—both make requests to CouchDB views and return collated results.

- How would you refactor the code in these APIs to minimize the amount of duplicate code?

  Hint: you don't need to fully grok the book-search code to identify what's different from field-search and how you could refactor out the parts that are the same.

400 Bad Request

In the lib/field-search.js file, we make a request to CouchDB by concatenating the base URL with the user-provided view:

```
url: config.bookdb + '_design/books/_view/by_' + req.params.view,
```

Notice that we use the req.params.view value without sanitizing it first. But we know that the only views we support are by author and by subject.

Change the code to inspect the incoming view string before concatenating it to make the URL. If the view isn't one of our expected values, respond with HTTP 400 Bad Request, including a JSON object explaining the problem.

DELETE

The book-bundle API we explored in this chapter has a method for adding a book to a bundle.

- How would you write an Express API endpoint for removing a book from a bundle with DELETE?

- What should your API do if the book isn't already in the bundle to begin with?

- What should your API do if the targeted bundle doesn't already exist?

The lib/bundle.js already has a REST endpoint for this. Take a look if you get stuck.

Promises and Deferreds

We used promises a lot in this chapter to manage success and failure cases for asynchronous requests, relying on the then() method to assign callbacks for when the promise is resolved or rejected. And we often sent array values to resolve promises (like [couchRes, body]).

Q implements the Promises/A specification.[6] Although this specification only requires a then() method, Q promises have more. For example, then() handlers always get one parameter, but Q's spread() method can handle multiple parameters.

- How would you change the API endpoints in this chapter to use spread() instead of then()?

- Was it the right choice to send array values to resolve promises? If not, what would you use instead?

---

6. http://wiki.commonjs.org/wiki/Promises/A

CHAPTER 7

Web Apps

By now, you've mastered several approaches to handling asynchronous JavaScript code. You know how to use and write RESTful web services. You understand messaging patterns, and how to use Express.

With all of that knowledge and experience, we're now in position to develop a web application. This will take us through the following Node.js aspects:

Architecture and Core

At this stage you've moved past the Node.js core in many respects. Node is the underlying technology that's letting you reach beyond.

Patterns

You'll dive deeper into Express middleware, using it to implement a custom authentication handler. We'll use passport—an Express plug-in—so that users of our application can log in with their Google accounts. The client-side code uses *model-view-controller* (MVC) to separate concerns.

JavaScriptisms

Although the Node code in this book takes advantage of the latest available ECMAScript Harmony features, those features aren't available in many web browsers. You'll learn some differences between ECMAScript 5 and ECMAScript 6 as we code JavaScript for the browser. You'll also use jQuery to perform a variety of client-side operations.

Supporting Code

Just like npm makes it easy to pull in Node modules, *Bower* is used to manage client-side dependencies. We'll use Bower to pull in jQuery, Bootstrap, Handlebars, and others. We'll also use Redis, a fast key-value store, for managing session data.

Developing web applications is an *enormous* topic. You could fill a library with books on all the myriad concepts you need to know to master it. I've been doing it for over a decade, and I'm still learning every day.

So instead of trying to explore everything there is to know, we'll focus on what's specific to Node.js. The code download that accompanies this book contains a web-app directory, which has all the code from this chapter and more. I encourage you to go grab it if you haven't already, since we won't cover everything that's in there.

The application b4 builds on the web services that we developed last chapter. This means you'll need CouchDB running, along with the data from Chapter 5, *Accessing Databases*, on page 65.

Once you have those prerequisites, let's dive in!

Storing Express Sessions in Redis

Whenever you have a user-facing web application, you'll almost always use sessions. A *session* is data that's attached to a particular user. As the user browses pages on the site or uses the web application, the server keeps track of the user through a *session cookie*. On each request, the server reads the cookie, retrieves the session data, then uses it when generating a response.

Exactly where you store this session data is up to you. By default, Express will keep the data in memory, but this doesn't readily scale. Once you have more than one Node.js process, the session data should really be stored to be in a shared place. That way, no matter which process services a user's request, it will have the correct information.

Let's see how to enable sessions in Express, and how to use Redis for storing the session data.

Enabling Sessions in Express

To enable sessions, add the cookieParser and session middleware to your app:

```
app.use(express.cookieParser());
app.use(express.session({ secret: 'unguessable' }));
```

The cookieParser middleware is responsible for parsing incoming cookies from the client, and the session middleware stores the session data attached to the cookie. The secret parameter is necessary to prevent cookie tampering and spoofing—set it to something unique to your application. Express session cookies are signed with this secret string.

Using Redis to Store Session Data

Redis is an extremely fast key/value store with tunable durability. This means you can keep it fast but risk losing data if the server were to crash, or you can sacrifice speed for greater durability guarantees.

By default, Redis keeps data in memory and then periodically writes it to disk. This makes it blazingly fast, but disaster-prone since a process crash would mean lost data.

Its speed makes Redis an ideal database for storing session data. If the server tips over, then the sessions might be lost, but at worst this means that your users will have to log in again.

To use Redis with your Node/Express app, first you'll have to install it. Installing Redis differs by platform, but once you have it installed, starting it up is a single command:

```
$ redis-server
...
[8344] 10 Sep 20:38:41.564 # Server started, Redis version 2.6.13
```

Using Redis with Express takes a couple of npm modules: redis and connect-redis. Run npm install --save to get them and add them to your package.json.

As an experiment, let's modify the server.js file from the last chapter's "Hello World" app to use Redis for session storage. Open the server.js file and add this to the const declarations at the top:

web-app/hello/server.js
```
redisClient = require('redis').createClient(),
RedisStore = require('connect-redis')(express),
```

The first line constructs a client for the Redis database. This will immediately open a TCP socket to your Redis server. The second line produces a class you can use to instantiate a Redis-based backing store for sessions.

Finally, in the middleware section of your server.js file, use the cookie and session middleware with Redis like so:

web-app/hello/server.js
```
app.use(express.cookieParser());
app.use(express.session({
  secret: 'unguessable',
  store: new RedisStore({
    client: redisClient
  })
}));
```

```
app.get('/api/:name', function(req, res) {
  res.json(200, { "hello": req.params.name });
});

app.listen(3000, function(){
  console.log("ready captain.");
});
```

Here we create a new instance of RedisStore based on our redisClient for the session middleware to use. With those changes in place, start up the server:

```
$ npm start

> hello@0.1.0 start ./hello
> node --harmony ./server.js

ready captain.
```

Then, in a second terminal, let's check out the HTTP headers with curl:

```
$ curl -i -X HEAD http://localhost:3000/api/test
HTTP/1.1 200 OK
X-Powered-By: Express
Content-Type: application/json; charset=utf-8
Content-Length: 21
Set-Cookie: connect.sid=s%3A-Coz4SVOKykt-fb5bTv7CHOj.IKL445JyFaKDq2aJ2%2FC95dh
            87pgElsNmc2mq3mpbjNE; Path=/; HttpOnly
Date: Fri, 27 Sep 2013 22:03:52 GMT
Connection: keep-alive
```

Notice the long Set-Cookie header—this is the session cookie. You can confirm that the data has been saved in Redis with the redis-cli command-line tool:

```
$ redis-cli KEYS 'sess:*'
1) "sess:-Coz4SVOKykt-fb5bTv7CHOj"
```

Here we've asked for all the keys in Redis that start with sess:—that is, the stored session data. Typically you won't go digging around in Redis for this data yourself, but it's helpful to confirm that everything is working.

Let's return now to the b4 application, which will use Redis for session storage in just this way. With Redis running, we can build a stateful web application on top our RESTful services.

Creating a Single-Page Web Application

A single-page web application consists of an HTML page, CSS to style it, and JavaScript to perform the application logic. All of these things can be delivered as static files, meaning they don't require any special server-side processing. You can just serve them up from the file system.

In this section, you'll see how to serve static content from Express alongside your RESTful APIs. Some of the static content will come from third-party dependencies, which we'll pull from Bower.

Serving Static Content with Express

Express comes with a convenient way to serve static files. All you have to do is use the express.static middleware and provide a directory. For example, these lines appear in the b4 server:

```
web-app/b4/server.js
app.use(express.static(__dirname + '/static'));
app.use(express.static(__dirname + '/bower_components'));
```

These two lines tell Express to serve static content out of the static/ and bower_components/ directories of the project. This means that if Express can't find a particular route, it'll fall back to serving the static content, checking these directories one at a time.

The static middleware is special in this regard. Most of the time, middleware has its effect in the middle of the request processing, but static appends its effect to the end of the chain (even after the route handlers have run).

For instance, the project's static/ directory contains three files: index.html, app.css, and app.js. These contain the HTML, CSS, and client-side JavaScript for the b4 application, respectively.

With the server running, when you request http://localhost:3000/index.html, Express will serve up static/index.html because we don't have an explicit route for it.

Installing Bower Components

Bower is a package manager for front-end code, like JavaScript libraries. You install Bower components in much the same way you install npm modules.

Here's the bower.json file from the b4 application:

```
web-app/b4/bower.json
{
  "name": "b4",
  "version": "0.0.1",
  "dependencies": {
    "jquery": "~2.0.3",
    "bootstrap": "~3.0.0",
    "typeahead.js": "~0.9.3",
    "typeahead.js-bootstrap.css": "*",
    "handlebars": "~1.0.0"
  }
}
```

Like a package.json file, it contains a list of dependencies. Our app depends on these front-end packages:

- jquery—Extraordinarily popular JavaScript library for Ajax and DOM manipulation

- bootstrap—Pretty CSS styles for web applications

- typeahead.js—JavaScript library for autocompleting text fields

- typeahead.js-bootstrap.css—Bootstrap-compatible CSS for typeahead.js

- handlebars—HTML templating library

To install these packages, first install Bower through npm (if you haven't already):

```
$ npm install -g bower
```

Then install the Bower components:

```
$ bower install
```

Now you should have a bower_components/ directory containing all of the above.

Structuring a Single-Page App

With the server ready to serve the static content, and Bower components in place, we can put together the main entry point of our single-page app: the index.html file. Here's what the top of that file contains:

web-app/b4/static/index.html
```html
<!doctype html>
<html>
<head>
  <meta charset="utf-8">
  <title>b4 - The Better Book Bundle Builder</title>
  <meta name="viewport" content="width=device-width, initial-scale=1.0">
  <link rel="stylesheet" href="bootstrap/dist/css/bootstrap.min.css">
  <link rel="stylesheet" href="bootstrap/dist/css/bootstrap-theme.min.css">
  <link rel="stylesheet"
      href="typeahead.js-bootstrap.css/typeahead.js-bootstrap.css">
  <link rel="stylesheet" href="app.css">
</head>
<body class="container">
```

The first line—<!doctype html>—tells the browser that this is an HTML5 document. Then we enter the document's <head> section, which contains the title, some <meta> tags, and a bunch of style sheets.

The viewport <meta> tag tells mobile devices that the width of the page should match the device width (e.g., 320px on an iPhone) instead of the default, which may be much larger. It also tells the device to start off at a scale of 1.0, meaning unzoomed.

The style sheets correspond to our dependencies; first the Bootstrap core and theme, then the typeahead styles, and finally our own app.css file. The app.css file comes last, so we can easily override any styles that may have come before.

The container class on the <body> element is a Bootstrapism. It tells Bootstrap to automatically grow or shrink the width of the body so it looks good at a variety of screen sizes.

Next, let's check out the bottom of index.html:

```
web-app/b4/static/index.html
    <script src="jquery/jquery.min.js"></script>
    <script src="bootstrap/dist/js/bootstrap.min.js"></script>
    <script src="typeahead.js/dist/typeahead.min.js"></script>
    <script src="handlebars/handlebars.js"></script>
    <script src="app.js"></script>
</body>
</html>
```

Like the head, this is where we bring in a bunch of dependencies and our own code. app.js is last so we can use all the other libraries in our application logic.

The vast middle of the index.html file contains the visual content of the application, such as templates for rendering views. We'll get to this, but before we do, we need a few more APIs.

Specifically, we need authenticated endpoints for doing user-specific actions. We'll develop those next, then return to the client side to pull it all together.

Authenticating with Passport

Passport is an Express plug-in that provides middleware for a variety of third-party logins. Using passport you can unobtrusively add support for logging in with Twitter, Facebook, and other services.

We're going to use passport to support authentication with Google credentials. Go get the passport and passport-google modules from npm if you don't have them already (npm install --save passport passport-google).

To add passport, first add this to your const declarations at the top of your server.js file:

```
web-app/b4/server.js
passport = require('passport'),
GoogleStrategy = require('passport-google').Strategy;
```

Then you need to initialize the passport middleware. Add this right after app.use(express.session...):

```
web-app/b4/server.js
app.use(passport.initialize());
app.use(passport.session());
```

Passport's different authentication mechanisms are called *strategies*. The second line in the previous code brings in the Google authentication strategy.

Configuring Passport Strategies

Passport itself and the strategies you use both require a bit of configuration to be useful. Here's a short example of how to configure passport with the Google strategy.

```
web-app/b4/server.js
passport.serializeUser(function(user, done) {
  done(null, user.identifier);
});
passport.deserializeUser(function(id, done) {
  done(null, { identifier: id });
});
```

This code sets up passport's serialization and deserialization functions and tells passport to use the Google strategy we pulled in earlier.

Use the serializeUser() method to specify what information about the user should actually be stored in the session. You can still keep other data elsewhere, but this is the data that gets associated with the session cookie.

Typically, you'll only store the minimum amount of information necessary to look up whatever else you need. Here, we're just storing the identifier string, which is a unique, user-specific URL provided by Google.

The deserializeUser() method is where you take the stored session data and turn it back into a rich object for use by your application. This operation must be light and fast since it will happen on virtually every request to your server. With the exception of some user-specific APIs we'll develop shortly, we don't need anything more than the identifier for our book-bundler app. So here we just construct an object containing the identifier we stored previously.

Next we tell passport to use() the Google strategy we brought in earlier:

```
web-app/b4/server.js
passport.use(new GoogleStrategy({
    returnURL: 'http://localhost:3000/auth/google/return',
    realm: 'http://localhost:3000/'
  },
  function(identifier, profile, done) {
    profile.identifier = identifier;
    return done(null, profile);
  }
));
```

The callback function is invoked once the authentication succeeds. This is your opportunity to grab any additional information tied to this user's account from your own database. Just like our deserializeUser() callback, we mainly make note of the identifier.

The returnURL parameter is the full URL you want Google to send users to after they've authenticated. Localhost is correct for our development application, but you'll need to set this to the real public URL of your own services.

Routing Authentication Requests

Finally, we need to set up some routes. We need to handle three kinds of requests in total: one for initiating the authentication, one for the returnURL where users come back after authenticating, and one for logging out.

Here's a small amount of code that provides these three endpoints:

```
web-app/b4/server.js
app.get('/auth/google/:return?',
  passport.authenticate('google', { successRedirect: '/' })
);
app.get('/auth/logout', function(req, res){
  req.logout();
  res.redirect('/');
});
```

The first route here works for both /auth/google and /auth/google/return. It uses the passport.authenticate() middleware, which will automatically redirect end users to Google's sign-in page and process the incoming token when they get back. In your own applications, you may want to take additional actions in either of these cases, but redirecting to the application root (/) is sufficient for our app.

Lastly, the /auth/logout route provides a way for users to clear out their session cookies and the associated session data.

That's all there is to it! It might seem like this is a lot of steps to get authentication to work. But it really is providing a lot of value—once you get passport set up, the job of authenticating users is done for you.

Authorizing APIs with Custom Middleware

With passport's Google strategy set up and Redis configured to store session information, we're in position to develop some protected user APIs. Unlike the book and bundle APIs we developed in the last chapter, these APIs will provide access to information specifically for logged-in users.

Here are the endpoints we'll create, and the HTTP verbs they'll support. They all return JavaScript Object Notation (JSON):

- /api/user (GET)—Basic information about the user (like the user's identifier)

- /api/user/bundles (GET)—Object that maps bundle IDs to bundle names

- /api/user/bundles (PUT)—Overwrites the bundle mapping object with the provided JSON body

Implementing these APIs will give us a chance to develop some custom Express middleware. We'll also have to modify our redisClient to be more tolerant of failures so we can report them through the API.

Tolerating Redis Errors

Redis is a fairly robust service, but like all things it can go down from time to time. For this reason, the connect-redis session plug-in is tolerant of Redis errors. Whenever Redis is unreachable, the plug-in will silently ignore it—in effect rendering your application sessionless, but otherwise unaffected.

We can do better. REST demands that we use the best HTTP status codes available to depict the state of the resource and the system serving it. To do that, we'll need to know more about what's going on with Redis.

Let's start by adding some nice logging with the npmlog module—the same one that npm uses for its colorful log messages. Use npm install to get it, then add this to your const declarations:

```
log = require('npmlog'),
```

Let's add some logging for key events to our redisClient:

web-app/b4/server.js
```
redisClient
  .on('ready', function() { log.info('REDIS', 'ready'); })
  .on('error', function(err) { log.error('REDIS', err.message); });
```

Here we're adding handlers for the ready event, which fires whenever Redis is connected and awaiting commands, and the error event. Handling the error event prevents Node from throwing an exception (recall that unhandled error events on EventEmitters throw). To see how this works, start up your b4 server then kill the redis-server process in another terminal. You'll see output like this:

```
$ npm start

> b4@0.1.0 start ./b4
> node --harmony ./server.js

ready captain.
info REDIS ready
ERR! REDIS Redis connection to 127.0.0.1:6379 failed - connect ECONNREFUSED
ERR! REDIS Redis connection to 127.0.0.1:6379 failed - connect ECONNREFUSED
```

The redisClient object includes a Boolean property ready, which we can check in our middleware. Let's do that next.

Implementing Custom Middleware

You've already learned how to implement route handlers in Express; now let's see how to create custom middleware. The difference between middleware and route handlers is that middleware is meant to be a link in the chain, while route handlers are meant to be at the very end of the chain. A middleware function takes three parameters: a request object (req), a response object (res), and a function (next) to call when the middleware is done.

Let's create a middleware function that enforces our passport session. If everything goes according to plan it'll call the next function, but if anything goes wrong it'll give an appropriate, RESTful response.

web-app/b4/server.js
```
const authed = function(req, res, next) {
  if (req.isAuthenticated()) {
    return next();
  } else if (redisClient.ready) {
    res.json(403, {
      error: "forbidden",
      reason: "not_authenticated"
    });
  } else {
    res.json(503, {
      error: "service_unavailable",
      reason: "authentication_unavailable"
    });
  }
};
```

First, we check req.isAuthenticated(). This is a method added by passport that returns true only if the incoming session cookie matches a known session. If the user is authenticated, we immediately call next() to move down the middleware chain.

Otherwise, find out if redisClient.ready is true. If it is, then the user truly isn't authenticated (not a system error) and the correct code is 403 Forbidden. We can't use 401 Unauthorized because that requires a WWW-Authenticate header, which tells the browser what authentication mechanisms are available (and there's no provision for cookie-based sessions).

Lastly, if redisClient.ready is false, then there's no way the user could have authenticated. The appropriate response is 503 Service Unavailable, since any authenticated APIs can't meaningfully operate until Redis comes back online.

Alright, now that we have custom middleware, let's apply it to some authenticated APIs.

Creating Authenticated APIs

We need to create new, user-specific APIs, and we want them to use our authed() middleware. But we certainly don't want all the other routes (like our static file serving) to be authenticated. Those still need to be served without any authentication. So we can't just call app.use() like we would with other middleware.

When you specify a route in Express, you can include middleware that you wish to apply to only that route. We'll use this feature for the /api/user route:

web-app/b4/server.js
```
app.get('/api/user', authed, function(req, res){
  res.json(req.user);
});
```

This short route handler is all we need, thanks to the authed() function we already made. By the time the route handler is invoked, the middleware has already confirmed that the session is valid and the user property on the request will have the right data.

Once logged in, requests to /api/user will return something like this:

```
{
  "identifier": "https://www.google.com/accounts/o8/id?id=..."
}
```

This is the object that comes out of the deserializeUser() callback we defined earlier. Next, let's see how to implement the /api/user/bundles endpoint:

web-app/b4/server.js
```
app.get('/api/user/bundles', authed, function(req, res) {
  let userURL = config.b4db + encodeURIComponent(req.user.identifier);
  request(userURL, function(err, couchRes, body) {
    if (err) {
      res.json(502, { error: "bad_gateway", reason: err.code });
    } else if (couchRes.statusCode === 200) {
      res.json(JSON.parse(body).bundles || {});
    } else {
      res.send(couchRes.statusCode, body);
    }
  });
});
```

First we construct a userURL, which consists of our CouchDB b4 database root and the identifier for the session. This implies a schema decision; the user documents in the b4 database will have same _id as the Google identifier. In your own applications you might want to use an app-specific ID for your users, but keep in mind that you'll need a mapping or lookup function to find users by their passport ID.

Next we call out to CouchDB using the request() function, as we've done many times before. We handle the various error conditions, and if we get back a 200 OK status, then we extract the bundles property from the document and send that back to the requester.

Putting the bundles hash back into the user document is only slightly trickier:

web-app/b4/server.js
```
app.put('/api/user/bundles', [authed, express.json()], function(req, res) {
  let userURL = config.b4db + encodeURIComponent(req.user.identifier);
  request(userURL, function(err, couchRes, body) {
    if (err) {
      res.json(502, { error: "bad_gateway", reason: err.code });
    } else if (couchRes.statusCode === 200) {
      let user = JSON.parse(body);
      user.bundles = req.body;
      request.put({ url: userURL, json: user }).pipe(res);
    } else if (couchRes.statusCode === 404) {
      let user = { bundles: req.body };
      request.put({ url: userURL,  json: user }).pipe(res);
    } else {
      res.send(couchRes.statusCode, body);
    }
  });
});
```

Notice that now we're providing two middleware functions in an array. First is the authed middleware that we used before, and second is express.json(). The built-in express.json middleware parses each incoming request's content body when the Content-Type header is set to application/json. This way, when we access req.body, it's already an object and not just a buffer.

After that, it's a pretty typical RESTful API. First we try to get the user object from CouchDB. If it already exists, we overwrite the bundles and put it back. If it doesn't already exist, we create a new document with those bundles and put it in. Error cases are handled in the usual way.

Note here that we're using the pipe() feature of the request module to send a response forward to res. The usage is quite similar to a basic Stream's pipe method, but operates on higher-level Request and Response objects.

That wraps up the server side of this application. Next let's finish up by exploring some of the client side.

Client-Side MVC

Throughout this chapter we've kept a clean delineation between the server-side code (RESTful, JSON APIs) and the client-side code (static HTML, CSS, and JavaScript). The benefit of this separation is that you can completely change your user-facing code without having to modify your Node server. In fact, you could implement a non-browser front end, such as a command-line interface, and your APIs would continue to work just fine.

But at some point you have to create an interface your users can interact with, and that's what we'll do here. Please keep in mind that front-end web development is a fast-moving target; the state of the art is advancing every day. To build a front end for the b4 APIs, we'll use MVC.

The MVC software-design pattern is a popular and convenient way to structure user-facing applications. Unfortunately, because it's so popular, people have different ideas about what MVC means and how it works. So first we have to agree on a working definition for the examples in this book.

- Model—The business logic and data for the application
- View—Representation of the model that is shown to the user
- Controller—Code that receives user interaction to inform the model

In our application, the model will be responsible for keeping track of the book bundles for the user. The view will be the Document Object Model (DOM) in the browser, as rendered by the model. And the controller logic will be invoked by events on the DOM.

Hash-Based Views

When a web application consists of only a single page, you need some way of denoting that different content is being shown. One way to do this is with URL *hashes*—the content after the # symbol in a URL.

For example, consider the URL http://localhost:3000/#list-bundles. We want this to correspond to the view that shows the user's bundles.

Open the static/index.html file in the b4 project. In there you'll find <div>s like this:

```
<div id="welcome-view" class="view">
  <h2>Welcome</h2>
  ...
</div>
<div id="list-bundles-view" class="view">
  <h2>Your Bundles</h2>
  ...
</div>
```

We want exactly one of these views visible at a time, and for that we need a little client-side JavaScript. Here's the showView() function from static/app.js:

```
web-app/b4/static/app.js
showView = function(selected) {
  window.location.hash = '#' + selected;
  $('.view').hide().filter('#' + selected + '-view').show();
},
```

This function takes a selected parameter, which is the name of the view we want to show. First we set window.location.hash to match the specified view. For example, if we call showView('list-bundles'), that updates the page's URL to end in #list-bundles.

The next part is pretty concise, thanks to jQuery. We find all of the <div>s on the page with class view, hide them, then find just the one whose ID matches our chosen view, and show it.

The showView() function works great if we want to set the view programmatically, but we should also respond to direct URL changes. To do that, we listen to the hashchange event on the window:

```
web-app/b4/static/app.js
$(window).on('hashchange', function(event){
  var view = (window.location.hash || '').replace(/^#/, '');
  if ($('#' + view + '-view').length) {
    showView(view);
  }
});
```

This code starts out by grabbing the window.location.hash and saving it in a variable called view. var is an older JavaScript keyword. It's just like let except that it's scoped to the nearest function(){} as opposed to the nearest pair of curly braces {}.

Not all browsers support let at the time of this writing, so it's much safer to use var in client-side code.

Next this function checks whether there's an element on the page with the matching view ID, and if so, calls showView().

Now there's only one more view-navigation task to take care of: what to do when the page first loads. On startup, the page should find out whether users are authenticated. If so, users should see the list-bundles view; otherwise, send them to the welcome view, where they'll have a link to log in.

Here's the startup view code:

```
web-app/b4/static/app.js
$.ajax({
  url: '/api/user',
  accepts: 'application/json'
})

.then(function(data, status, xhr) {
  getBundles();
}, function(xhr, status, err) {
  showView('welcome');
});
```

First, we kick off an asynchronous request /api/user with jQuery's $.ajax(). This method is like a promise-producing request().

We call then() with two handlers, one for success and one for failure. If the request was successful, we move on to getBundles(); otherwise we show the user the welcome view.

Next, let's look at some more client-side request code.

Synchronizing Models with REST APIs

In our single-page web app, once the user logs in he'll see the list-bundles view. But before we can render it, we need to know what bundles the user has already made.

The static/app.js file in the b4 project contains a variable called bundles. This is a local copy of the actual user bundles stored on the server. To start, the web app needs to pull down the remote copy—this is what getBundles() does:

web-app/b4/static/app.js

```
getBundles = function() {
  $.ajax({
    url: '/api/user/bundles'
  })
  .then(function(data, status, xhr) {
    bundles = data;
    showBundles();
  }, function(xhr, status, err) {
    if (xhr.status >= 500) {
      showErr(xhr, status, err);
    }
    bundles = {};
    showBundles();
  });
},
```

Here we use the $.ajax() function to pull down /api/user/bundles. If the request succeeds, we use the value returned; otherwise we start with an empty object ({}). If the request fails with a status code in the 500 range (like 502 Bad Gateway), then we show the error using the showErr() function. In either case, we move on to showBundles(). Going the other direction, we have a saveBundles() function that saves the bundles on the server:

web-app/b4/static/app.js

```
saveBundles = function(bundles, callback) {
  $.ajax({
    type: 'PUT',
    url: '/api/user/bundles',
    data: JSON.stringify(bundles),
    contentType: 'application/json; charset=utf-8',
    accepts: 'application/json'
  })
  .then(function(data, status, xhr) {
    callback(null, data);
  }, function(xhr, status, err) {
    callback(err);
  });
},
```

This function takes a bundles object to push, and a Node-style callback function that will be called on success or failure. It uses $.ajax() to PUT the bundles object up to /api/user/bundles. The contentType option indicates that the data is already pre-serialized as JSON and doesn't require form encoding.

That covers the client-side code for interacting with the user APIs we developed this chapter. The b4 app contains similar code for using the APIs we developed in previous chapters—like the book-search and bundle-modification APIs. Now let's produce a user interface for our data.

Generating HTML with Handlebars

The b4 app uses *templates* for generating HTML from input data. A template is basically HTML with holes where data will get filled in. There are many of JavaScript templating engines to choose from—this app uses Handlebars.[1]

Handlebars replaces named tokens in a source string with values from a context object. It also supports looping over objects and arrays, and conditional logic (if/else). For example, here's the Handlebars template for generating a table to display a user's list of bundles:

```
web-app/b4/static/index.html
<table class="table">
  <thead>
    <tr>
      <th>Bundle Name</th>
      <th class="actions">Actions</th>
    </tr>
  </thead>
  <tbody>
    {{#each bundles}}
    <tr data-id="{{@key}}">
      <td>{{this}}</td>
      <td class="actions">
        <button type="button" class="btn edit">
          <abbr title="edit bundle" class="glyphicon glyphicon-pencil">
            <span>edit bundle</span>
          </abbr>
        </button>
        <button type="button" class="btn delete">
          <abbr title="delete bundle" class="glyphicon glyphicon-trash">
            <span>delete bundle</span>
          </abbr>
        </button>
      </td>
    </tr>
    {{/each}}
  </tbody>
</table>
```

Starting on line 9, we loop over the bundles object. For each key/value pair, we add a <tr> whose data-id attribute is set to the current key. And inside that row we add a <td> element with the text set to the current value ({{this}}).

Our b4 app compiles and executes the Handlebars templates entirely on the client side, but you can push some or all of these tasks to the server since Handlebars can run in Node.js as well.

---

1.   http://handlebarsjs.com/

For example, you could compile the templates in Node, and then just perform the data replacement in the browser. Or you could perform the data replacement in Node too, and serve up HTML chunks instead of JSON. Each of these options has advantages depending on your particular application.

Wrapping Up

This chapter showed both sides of web application development, from the Node.js server out to the browser. It took us further into web services as we developed stateful, session-based user APIs. And we used Redis, a fast key/value datastore for housing our session data in a scalable way.

By bringing in passport—an Express plug-in—we provided seamless support for logging in with Google credentials. And we developed custom Express middleware to authorize requests to our RESTful user APIs.

To power the client side, we served static content, both for our single-page application itself and its dependencies, which we got from Bower, an un-opinionated front-end package manager. We used jQuery's Ajax capabilities to synchronize our model objects with our REST services, and its DOM-manipulation functions to implement custom hash-based views. Lastly, we explored templating with Handlebars as part of implementing client-side MVC.

RESTful API Design

Consider the user-bundles API (/api/user/bundles) we designed in this chapter. On PUT, it always overwrites the whole list of bundles whenever any of them change.

- What would happen if the incoming response body weren't valid JSON?

- What would happen if the incoming response body were a JSON serialized array (as opposed to the object that we expect)?

- In your opinion, what should ideally happen in these cases, and how would you change the code to make that so?

Instead of just using PUT to overwrite everything, you could have different verbs and endpoints for adding and deleting bundles from a user's collection.

- What route would you use to DELETE a bundle from a user's collection?

- What HTTP verb would you use to add a bundle to a user's collection?

Parting Thoughts

By now you've learned quite a bit about how to use Node for both web and non-web server-side JavaScript projects. Node.js is inherently asynchronous —and while this may have been unfamiliar to you to begin with, you've learned several techniques for managing asynchronous JavaScript code.

You've used Node.js to implement middleware applications that perform a variety of tasks, from seeding databases with information to doling out work to a cluster of worker processes. You've developed custom protocols and worked with familiar ones like HTTP. You have made RESTful web services as well as services that use other communication patterns such as push/pull and publish/subscribe.

Along the way, you learned how to use a number of useful npm modules. You used Express for simplifying the development of REST endpoints, and node-unit for running unit tests on your data processing code. The request module was super useful for making HTTP requests, and async and Q made managing asynchronous code flows easier (each in their own way).

The world of Node.js is still expanding rapidly. There are lots of ways to attack any given problem, and there's always someone out there trying it in a new way. As you go forward and develop your own style, keep your eyes and ears open for new approaches and new techniques. It's an exciting time to be a Node developer.

Good luck, and happy coding!

The Modern Web

Get up to speed on the latest HTML, CSS, and JavaScript techniques.

HTML5 and CSS3 (2nd edition)

HTML5 and CSS3 are more than just buzzwords—
they're the foundation for today's web applications.
This book gets you up to speed on the HTML5 elements
and CSS3 features you can use right now in your current projects, with backwards compatible solutions
that ensure that you don't leave users of older browsers
behind. This new edition covers even more new features, including CSS animations, IndexedDB, and
client-side validations.

Brian P. Hogan
(300 pages) ISBN: 9781937785598. $38
http://pragprog.com/book/bhh52e

Async JavaScript

With the advent of HTML5, front-end MVC, and
Node.js, JavaScript is ubiquitous—and still messy.
This book will give you a solid foundation for managing
async tasks without losing your sanity in a tangle of
callbacks. It's a fast-paced guide to the most essential
techniques for dealing with async behavior, including
PubSub, evented models, and Promises. With these
tricks up your sleeve, you'll be better prepared to
manage the complexity of large web apps and deliver
responsive code.

Trevor Burnham
(104 pages) ISBN: 9781937785277. $17
http://pragprog.com/book/tbajs

Put the "Fun" in Functional

Elixir puts the "fun" back into functional programming, on top of the robust, battle-tested, industrial-strength environment of Erlang.

Programming Elixir

You want to explore functional programming, but are put off by the academic feel (tell me about monads just one more time). You know you need concurrent applications, but also know these are almost impossible to get right. Meet Elixir, a functional, concurrent language built on the rock-solid Erlang VM. Elixir's pragmatic syntax and built-in support for metaprogramming will make you productive and keep you interested for the long haul. This book is *the* introduction to Elixir for experienced programmers.

Dave Thomas
(240 pages) ISBN: 9781937785581. $36
http://pragprog.com/book/elixir

Programming Erlang (2nd edition)

A multi-user game, web site, cloud application, or networked database can have thousands of users all interacting at the same time. You need a powerful, industrial-strength tool to handle the really hard problems inherent in parallel, concurrent environments. You need Erlang. In this second edition of the best-selling *Programming Erlang*, you'll learn how to write parallel programs that scale effortlessly on multicore systems.

Joe Armstrong
(548 pages) ISBN: 9781937785536. $42
http://pragprog.com/book/jaerlang2

The Joy of Math and Healthy Programming

Rediscover the joy and fascinating weirdness of pure mathematics, and learn how to take a healthier approach to programming.

Good Math

Mathematics is beautiful—and it can be fun and exciting as well as practical. *Good Math* is your guide to some of the most intriguing topics from two thousand years of mathematics: from Egyptian fractions to Turing machines; from the real meaning of numbers to proof trees, group symmetry, and mechanical computation. If you've ever wondered what lay beyond the proofs you struggled to complete in high school geometry, or what limits the capabilities of the computer on your desk, this is the book for you.

Mark C. Chu-Carroll
(282 pages) ISBN: 9781937785338. $34
http://pragprog.com/book/mcmath

The Healthy Programmer

To keep doing what you love, you need to maintain your own systems, not just the ones you write code for. Regular exercise and proper nutrition help you learn, remember, concentrate, and be creative—skills critical to doing your job well. Learn how to change your work habits, master exercises that make working at a computer more comfortable, and develop a plan to keep fit, healthy, and sharp for years to come.

This book is intended only as an informative guide for those wishing to know more about health issues. In no way is this book intended to replace, countermand, or conflict with the advice given to you by your own healthcare provider including Physician, Nurse Practitioner, Physician Assistant, Registered Dietician, and other licensed professionals.

Joe Kutner
(254 pages) ISBN: 9781937785314. $36
http://pragprog.com/book/jkthp

Sound and Games

Add live sound to your apps, and explore a faster way of building mobile games for Android and iOS.

Programming Sound with Pure Data

Sound gives your native, web, or mobile apps that extra dimension, and it's essential for games. Rather than using canned samples from a sample library, learn how to build sounds from the ground up and produce them for web projects using the Pure Data programming language. Even better, you'll be able to integrate dynamic sound environments into your native apps or games—sound that reacts to the app, instead of sounding the same every time. Start your journey as a sound designer, and get the power to craft the sound you put into your digital experiences.

Tony Hillerson
(200 pages) ISBN: 9781937785666. $36
http://pragprog.com/book/thsound

Create Mobile Games with Corona

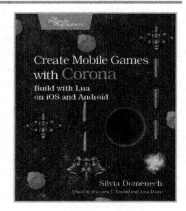

Develop cross-platform mobile games with Corona using the Lua programming language! Corona is experiencing explosive growth among mobile game developers, and this book gets you up to speed on how to use this versatile platform. You'll use the Corona SDK to simplify game programming and take a fun, no-nonsense approach to write and add must-have gameplay features. You'll find out how to create all the gaming necessities: menus, sprites, movement, perspective and sound effects, levels, loading and saving, and game physics. Along the way, you'll learn about Corona's API functions and build three common kinds of mobile games from scratch that can run on the iPhone, iPad, Kindle Fire, Nook Color, and all other Android smartphones and tablets.

Printed in full color.

Silvia Domenech
(220 pages) ISBN: 9781937785574. $36
http://pragprog.com/book/sdcorona

Long Live the Command Line!

Use tmux and Vim for incredible mouse-free productivity.

tmux

Your mouse is slowing you down. The time you spend context switching between your editor and your consoles eats away at your productivity. Take control of your environment with tmux, a terminal multiplexer that you can tailor to your workflow. Learn how to customize, script, and leverage tmux's unique abilities and keep your fingers on your keyboard's home row.

Brian P. Hogan
(88 pages) ISBN: 9781934356968. $16.25
http://pragprog.com/book/bhtmux

Practical Vim

Vim is a fast and efficient text editor that will make you a faster and more efficient developer. It's available on almost every OS—if you master the techniques in this book, you'll never need another text editor. In more than 100 Vim tips, you'll quickly learn the editor's core functionality and tackle your trickiest editing and writing tasks.

Drew Neil
(346 pages) ISBN: 9781934356982. $29
http://pragprog.com/book/dnvim

The Pragmatic Bookshelf

The Pragmatic Bookshelf features books written by developers for developers. The titles continue the well-known Pragmatic Programmer style and continue to garner awards and rave reviews. As development gets more and more difficult, the Pragmatic Programmers will be there with more titles and products to help you stay on top of your game.

Visit Us Online

This Book's Home Page
http://pragprog.com/book/jwnode
Source code from this book, errata, and other resources. Come give us feedback, too!

Register for Updates
http://pragprog.com/updates
Be notified when updates and new books become available.

Join the Community
http://pragprog.com/community
Read our weblogs, join our online discussions, participate in our mailing list, interact with our wiki, and benefit from the experience of other Pragmatic Programmers.

New and Noteworthy
http://pragprog.com/news
Check out the latest pragmatic developments, new titles and other offerings.

Save on the eBook

Save on the eBook versions of this title. Owning the paper version of this book entitles you to purchase the electronic versions at a terrific discount.

PDFs are great for carrying around on your laptop—they are hyperlinked, have color, and are fully searchable. Most titles are also available for the iPhone and iPod touch, Amazon Kindle, and other popular e-book readers.

Buy now at *http://pragprog.com/coupon*

Contact Us

Online Orders:	*http://pragprog.com/catalog*
Customer Service:	*support@pragprog.com*
International Rights:	*translations@pragprog.com*
Academic Use:	*academic@pragprog.com*
Write for Us:	*http://pragprog.com/write-for-us*
Or Call:	+1 800-699-7764

CPSIA information can be obtained at www.ICGtesting.com
Printed in the USA
BVOW09s0956080316

439496BV00014B/67/P